The
Enneagram Relationship
Workbook

Other Books by Margaret Frings Keyes

Emotions and the Enneagram:
Working Through Your Shadow Life Script
Molysdatur Publications, Muir Beach, California 1990

The Enneagram Cats of Muir Beach
Molysdatur Publications, Muir Beach, California 1990

Inward Journey: Art as Therapy
Open Court Publishing Co., La Salle, Illinois
(revised edition 1983)

Staying Married
Les Femmes Publications, Millbrae, California 1975

Cartoons and drawings by M.K. Brown have appeared in anthologies, television, international film festivals and exhibitions, as well as her books published by Macmillan, Crown, and Scholastic.
Her work has been featured in the following magazines: *National Lampoon, Playboy, Mother Jones, Atlantic Monthly, Harper's, Women's Sports, Arcade Comics, Playgirl, Oui, Esquire, Berkeley Monthly, New West, Lear's, Wimmen's Comics, and California Magazine.*

THE ENNEAGRAM RELATIONSHIP WORKBOOK

A Self and Partnership Assessment Guide

Margaret Frings Keyes

Drawings by M. K. Brown

Molysdatur Publications
Muir Beach, California 94965
1992

ISBN: 1-882042-08-5
Library of Congress Card Catalog Number: 91-075330

The opinions expressed in this book are those of the author. They are not
derived from, and do not represent the teachings of any institution or school.
The characters, while based on real-life incidents, do not represent any persons,
living or dead.

Molysdatur Books are distributed by Publishers Services,
P.O. Box 2510, Novato, California 94948

Cover Art and illustrations by Mary K. Brown
Book design by Andrea DuFlon
Author's photograph by Michelle Vignes
Printed by Malloy Lithographing, Inc., Ann Arbor, Michigan

Some of the cartoons in this book have appeared in the following periodicals:
National Lampoon, Mother Jones, Lear's, and the *Berkeley Monthly.*

This book is for my godchildren
— pioneers and volunteers.

Contents

User-Friendly: Find what you want and move around.
Skip what you know already.

Part II. The Partnership Path to Self-Knowledge

List of Charts

Acknowledgments

Many people have written this book with me. Without those who gave me permission to use excerpts from their stories and my fellow Muir Beach writers who patiently went through the rewriting phases — Leba Wine, Jo Gros-Balthazard, and Judith Yamamoto — I could not have created this book. Equally important were those who pushed for more examples and greater clarity. Sally Tantau, Eliza Wingate, Joanne and Jack Buckley, Pen Bevan, Sandy Borgrink, and Scott O'Keefe were invaluable resources at the right moment. Audrey Fain's doctoral dissertation, "A Study of Couples Using the Enneagram," and John Destein's book *Coming Together, Coming Apart* influenced my thought about couples. Linda Remy, Adrienne Sciutto, and novelist Donna Levin critiqued my manuscript.

This workbook supplements *Emotions and the Enneagram* and continues my primary goal to provide further insight into Enneagram concepts of personality in the light of Jungian psychology. Readers interested in the occult and esoteric origins of the Enneagram or the Enneagon theories of Oscar Ichazo are referred to the Arica Institute in New York City. This Jungian view of the Ennea-types would probably be considered a distortion rather than an extension of Enneagon theory by Aricans.

Preface

The Author's Overview of How to Use This Book.

The most valuable exercise I know in psychotherapy, role reversal, allows us to visit and experience the different worlds of other people. We break free from a space suit of our own personality and look through another person's eyes. We not only see, but hear and *feel* that person's separate experience of his or her world — and of us.

An Enneagram workbook based in role play can broaden what we perceive about ourselves and other people. Looking at *what's so* in our lives in specific, concrete situations is the most practical way of identifying our compulsions. Looking at these same issues through the eyes of a different person gives us a whole set of new information. We have options for change that we ordinarily would not consider.

In role play, as in drama, we enact a present, past, or future circumstance. We enter a character's thoughts and feelings, then speak and act from that person's viewpoint. We learned to do this as children when we played dress-up in our parents' old clothes. Role reversal simply means that we look at the world through someone else's eyes for awhile, and they look at the world through ours. We can learn to do this with marriage partners, business associates, our parent of the past, even the children we once were. We are not restricted to present time.

Enlightenment, the "waking-up" sought through Enneagram study, involves the full development of various capacities — compassion, intelligence, creativity, and spontaneity. Role play and role reversal include and exercise them all.

This manual encourages the reader to acquire a taste for enlightenment by consciously entering into states of mind that may be quite different from his or her own. It includes techniques (and critiques) of self-assessment, exercises and information, and an added dimension — the cartoons of M.K. Brown — that highlights character in ways that words alone cannot.

Role play switches our point of view. Cartoons do also. They are a most powerful art form when used with skill. The cartoonist shows our hidden frame of reference by carrying it to an absurd but logical conclusion. The cartoon gets under our defenses. If someone tries to tell us about our behavior, we may feel threatened. But if we see it in a cartoon we sense its truth. For example, consider the Grand Canyon illustration. M.K. Brown's cartoon shows a couple standing beside the Grand Canyon. The woman, with a sour look on her face, remarks to her husband, "So that's the Grand Canyon." The Grand Canyon has shrunk to the size of a ditch. The husband stands frozen. We do not need to be told this woman has emasculated her husband. Her words have SHRUNK THE GRAND CANYON! Her life stance of critical assessment says "This (whatever) does not measure up to my idea of a perfect (whatever)." The comment withers all life, dries up all juice in the moment. Next time, if we catch ourselves before "ONE-ishly" rejecting something or someone out of hand, the cartoon may have done its work.

The manual begins with a Table of Contents that works a bit like a "user-friendly" computer menu. You do not have to deal with things you already know. On the other hand, readers completely unfamiliar with the Enneagram or modern psychology can choose chapters most useful to them. A self-assessment checklist is included for those who wish to identify their Enneagram point.

The heart of the book is the role-play and reversal chapter. The reader enters the mind-set of each of the nine Enneagram personality types through *active imagination* exercises. The exercises develop and train the reader's role-play skills and ability to empathize with responses different from his or her own. For example, imagine coming home from work finding the house empty and the living room furniture buried under athletic

So that's the Grand Canyon.

equipment. As an Enneagram ONE character, you might fume because the place is in such disorder. As an Enneagram FIVE, you might feel relieved that the family is away and you will have time to work on your own projects for a change. As an Enneagram SIX, you will probably worry that some catastrophe has occurred.

To help get a picture of each Enneagram personality, examples from movies, TV sitcoms, books, and some popular cartoons are given. Television characters show their relationship habits week after week. They rarely change and therefore can be superb examples to show the *patterned traits* of an Enneagram type. Once we recognize the pattern, we can see it in friends, family, and ourselves.

Linking Jungian psychology to Enneagram theory identifies a process of understanding that develops over a lifetime. Work with one's rejected "element of transformation" is essential. The process is most readily seen in life partnerships and vocations that demand total commitment.

The second part of the book deals with personal relationships. Partnership, particularly marriage, offers great help on the path to self-knowledge. Marriage tempers our spirit in a complex set of tasks. Its stages parallel the *individuation* process outlined by Carl G. Jung. Whether called enlightenment or individuation, the goal is to acquire an essential wholeness of mind, body, and spirit.

The workbook description of each of the four stages of partnership includes exercises to help the reader delve into his or her own life. This section can be done alone or working with a partner.

Finally, the book touches on the broad world of group relationships. What blocks and what eases the flow of relationship? What does it have to do with the massive cultural shift occurring as we approach the 21st century? Parallel Enneagram processes occur in both the individual and the group. The final segment suggests some directions for further study.

A premise of this book is that we can shift from the narrow, defensive points of view acquired in childhood to a level of compassionate empathy. We can understand and love one another through understanding our differences. Despite the several *at-a-glance* study charts, there is no intention to represent the necessary daily work as easy. Still, a map helps.

PART I.
SELF ASSESSMENT

Introduction
to the Enneagram

The Enneagram, a geometric symbol, refers to nine basic personality types and their interrelationships. Although the system is said to have developed in the Arab world among the Sufis, the name comes from the Greek words *ennea*, meaning "nine," and *gram* meaning graph or drawing. The Enneagram describes nine personality types with their different opinions about reality.

Early in life children learn about rewards and punishment in the environment. They produce particular sets of behavior patterns, open and hidden traits and tendencies, that are predictable over time.

Each of the nine essential patterns reflected by the Enneagram represents a basic survival strategy and an appropriate response to the child's life circumstances. This point of view, like a window through which one glimpses only a part of reality, leads the child to interpret events during the rest of his or her life in its light. The child identifies with the small window frame of reference. Flexible or inflexible personality responses come from the *degree* of stress and threat experienced in early life. The more spontaneous in behavior and open to other points of view the child is, the healthier the adult will be.

Children need protection while they take the risks they need to grow. Otherwise they can be easily overwhelmed and develop rigid behaviors to protect themselves. There is a high correlation between the care our society takes of its children and the health of our people.

When we reject or do not see other points of view, we behave automatically from a defense-conditioned framework, somewhat like a robot or as if half asleep. Basic goals of human behavior — survival, pleasure, and relationships — become distorted. We pursue them in fixated shadow ways, contaminated with excessive desire and hatred.

Each of us carries some distortion based on what was missing or overvalued in our early lives. Classical novels — *The Brothers Karamazov, Anna Karenina, David Copperfield* — explore these themes. Our distorted perceptions and choices we make from these viewpoints correspond to what religion used to call the capital or deadly sins. It is intriguing but we also can look at the distortions as nine different forms of the Shadow archetype identified by Carl G. Jung. The Shadow, the first archetype we encounter when we start the process of waking up, mirrors our unpleasant truths. We must learn to include and integrate its many points of view.

Role play and role reversal, terms from psychodrama, refer to a special process of finding the windows used by our partners and others around us, including our "enemies." We learn to look from their windows into their reality, to see the world as they see it. Our understanding shifts and broadens.

The cartoons and written exercises of this workbook help us to switch perspective. They can enlarge our perception.

Before we reverse roles, however, we must observe our own inner behavior objectively. In psychotherapy and other systems of emotional discipline, we learn to distance ourselves from our thoughts and feelings without suppressing them. We then regain choice over our programmed responses. The process is identical to that taken on a spiritual path. We want to get rid of the partial (and therefore inaccurate) judgments we made as children.

Often in this culture, we first do a lot of angry blaming of others who got us into our fix. Old patterns become disrupted. We're uncomfortable — and everyone close to us is also uncomfortable.

Regardless of discomfort, if we have the courage to begin, a more open-minded understanding comes as we work. We see that our parents, family members, church leaders, and teachers were all just human beings looking at life from their limited points of view. Our problem partner, friend, child, or colleague is doing the same today.

As we free ourselves from emotional habits, we gain tolerance. We realize we cannot change or be responsible for the way the other person in our life views the world and the way he or she acts. When alibis from fear of blame or hurt lessen, communication between us opens. Compassion grows when we risk showing our feelings, and trust comes with practice. We are not talking about "bolt-of-lightning satori," but the bit-by-bit change of habits to which we are quite attached.

We learn our particular Enneagram point, then we learn not to overidentify with it. Humor and a sense of amusement grow. Awareness continues to deepen as we observe that we are part of the oneness of everything. Other stages in the deepening spiritual life, not the concern of this book, are discussed in the spiritual classics of various traditions. Contemporary beginning books include Evelyn Underhill's *Practical Mysticism* and Matthew Fox's books on creation theology.

The next section develops information to use with the chart *Enneagram Personalities At-A-Glance*. We then move into the active imagination exercises of role play to deepen our understanding of the Enneagram patterns.

1   \ \\\\ = 5
2   \ \\   = 3
3   \ \ \ \ = 4
4   \ \ \ \ = 4
5   \ \   = 2
6   \ \ \   = 3
7   \ \ \ \ \ = 5
8   \   = 1
          = 0
9   \\\\   = 4
0

1-7-3-4-0

2

Self-Assessment

An Enneagram Personality Checklist of 100 Items
— an easy scoring guide.

You begin study of the Enneagram with yourself. It is not easy. You know so many things about you. How do you give more weight to one set of traits over another? Then, once you have decided or been helped to discover your type, what, if anything, do you want to do about it? What should you focus on first — and why?

The following checklist will provide you with some data to use in the next exercises and a beginning sense of your point location on the Enneagram.

Check each number to the extent you agree with it as a description of you.

Agreement

Strong Some None

☒ ☐ ☐ 01. When I'm in the fast lane of a supermarket I always count the number of items in the next person's carry-out basket.

☐ ☒ ☐ 02. I expect my husband/wife, my kids, my friends, to know what I need without being told.

☒ ☐ ☐ 03. I'm an achiever, competent, and efficient; I want to be seen as such.

☒ ☐ ☐ 04. I'm excited by the extraordinary, the intense, and dramatic. I'm bored by the mundane and ordinary.

Strong	Some	None		
☒	☐	☐	05.	I hold on to what I have.
☐	☐	☒	06.	I'm often torn by doubt.
☐	☒	☐	07.	There are few situations in which I can't find something to enjoy.
☐	☒	☐	08.	I relish opposition.
☐	☐	☒	09.	I'm not a "self-starter."
☐	☐	☒	10.	Having enough to eat, a roof over my head, and my needs met is basic to everything else.
☐	☒	☐	11.	I do my assigned tasks as perfectly as possible, and I expect others to do their work in a similar way.
☐	☒	☐	12.	How I'm seen by important people is critical to me.
☐	☒	☐	13.	I know how to "market" myself.
☒	☐	☐	14.	I have a nostalgic feeling for incidents in my past.
☐	☐	☒	15.	I have trouble reaching out or asking for help from others.
☐	☐	☒	16.	I'm basically a middle-of-the-road person.
☐	☐	☒	17.	I wish other people would lighten up more.
☐	☐	☒	18.	I see the weak points in others. I know where to get at them if I need to.
☐	☒	☐	19.	Most things in life, if you think of them ten years from now, aren't worth getting upset about.
☐	☒	☐	20.	It's essential to me to feel needed and of central importance to my partner.
☐	☒	☐	21.	I take responsibility seriously and put out more effort than others do.
☐	☐	☒	22.	I'm a happy, giving person but, when offended, can turn into an aggressive fury.
☒	☐	☐	23.	Taking initiative in working with a team is easy for me.
☒	☐	☐	24.	Tasteful design in furniture, clothing, even machinery, is of utmost importance to me.
☐	☒	☐	25.	I'm bored by small talk and prefer time alone.
☐	☐	☒	26.	I have difficulty finishing tasks, whether it's work for an academic degree or cleaning house.

Strong Some None

☒ ☐ ☐ 27. Whenever a current project's difficulties are close to solved, I begin to look for something else to plan.

☐ ☐ ☒ 28. I don't trust my soft side.

☐ ☒ ☐ 29. I don't think of myself as being all that important.

☒ ☐ ☐ 30. I'm a survivor, and no matter what happens I'll make it.

☒ ☐ ☐ 31. I often feel more irritation at others' behavior than I express.

☒ ☐ ☐ 32. Others see me as warm and empathetic.

☐ ☒ ☐ 33. Dressing well allows me to be seen, heard, and to get things done.

☒ ☐ ☐ 34. Doing things well and with class matters greatly to me.

☐ ☐ ☒ 35. I prefer to watch rather than to interact with people.

☒ ☐ ☐ 36. It's very important not to make the wrong decision.

☐ ☒ ☐ 37. If a little is good, more is better.

☒ ☐ ☐ 38. I think other people create their own problems.

☐ ☐ ☒ 39. I don't like a job that requires endless decisions.

☒ ☐ ☐ 40. Getting or losing a relationship bothers me immensely.

☐ ☒ ☐ 41. I'm a fairly good critic because I can *always* see what is wrong or out of place.

☐ ☒ ☐ 42. I'm emotionally impulsive and love to be pampered.

☐ ☐ ☒ 43. Sometimes I feel my accomplishments mask the rest of me from being seen.

☐ ☐ ☒ 44. My surroundings deeply influence my moods and interest in work.

☐ ☐ ☒ 45. I like my solitude.

☒ ☐ ☐ 46. Sometimes the best approach to danger is a strong offense. but I'm aware of an edge of fear inside.

☒ ☐ ☐ 47. I'm unusually enthusiastic about people, possibilities, and the future.

☐ ☒ ☐ 48. How I view justice and injustice is the key to how I will act.

☐ ☐ ☒ 49. I generally follow the line of least resistance.

☐ ☐ ☒ 50. I tend to be more of a taker than a giver.

Strong	Some	None		
☒	☐	☐	51.	I'm generally meticulous and self-disciplined about details.
☐	☐	☒	52.	I expect my lover (partner or friend) to understand my needs and take care of them.
☒	☐	☐	53.	I work fast and efficiently.
☐	☒	☐	54.	Some people accuse me of being aloof.
☒	☐	☐	55.	I make my own decisions and work things out in my own way.
☐	☐	☒	56.	Before making a decision I get all the data I can to prepare, but often it is still difficult.
☐	☒	☐	57.	Most of the time I avoid getting into heavy issues.
☐	☒	☐	58.	I won't allow myself to be, or feel, cornered.
☐	☐	☒	59.	I have trouble listening and paying attention.
☒	☐	☐	60.	Nothing matters more in my life than my primary relationship.
☐	☒	☐	61.	When I find fault others are uneasy, but my intent is constructive.
☐	☐	☒	62.	I don't like routines, discipline, or having to account for things; how I feel is more important than what I do.
☒	☐	☐	63.	The right network of friends is important to my work.
☐	☐	☒	64.	I identify with elite standards and often feel others misunderstand them.
☐	☐	☒	65.	I use my privacy to think about projects and things that interest me.
☒	☐	☐	66.	I prefer to be with people much like myself.
☒	☐	☐	67.	I'm a list-maker of things to do, contacts, and possibilities.
☐	☐	☒	68.	It is easy for me to say no and to express my boredom.
☐	☐	☒	69.	I hate to waste my energy on anything. I wonder why rich people get out of bed in the morning.
☒	☐	☐	70.	I'm highly involved in social causes.
☒	☐	☐	71.	I'm always aware of what should and ought to be done.
☒	☐	☐	72.	Being attractive and lively is basic to my self esteem.
☐	☒	☐	73.	Others might describe me as a workaholic.

Strong	Some	None		
☐	☐	☒	74.	I'm rarely spontaneous.
☐	☐	☒	75.	I avoid social events whenever possible.
☐	☐	☒	76.	I seem to sense danger and threat more than others do.
☒	☐	☐	77.	One thing is barely finished before I look for the next interesting project.
☐	☐	☒	78.	I get what I want and use intimidation if necessary.
☐	☒	☐	79.	There is nothing so urgent that it can't wait until tomorrow.
☐	☒	☐	80.	Sex is my strongest drive.
☒	☐	☐	81.	Norms of behavior allow true freedom rather than chaos, and we should uphold them at all costs.
☐	☒	☐	82.	Children and others who need nurturing and protection appeal to me more than anything else.
☒	☐	☐	83.	I like applause, high-performance evaluations, and awards of all kinds.
☐	☐	☒	84.	Symbols appeal to me.
☐	☐	☒	85.	I'm silent, attentive, and let others take the initiative in most situations.
☐	☐	☒	86.	I identify with the underdog in most situations.
☒	☐	☐	87.	I'm involved with many things, many people, and have something going on all the time.
☐	☐	☒	88.	I make my own rules; you can take it or leave it.
☐	☒	☐	89.	I act as an advocate rather than an adversary and I calm situations down.
☐	☒	☐	90.	I tend to be passionate about social and political issues.
☐	☒	☐	91.	I evaluate and judge my own and others' behavior.
☐	☒	☐	92.	People often come to me for comfort and advice.
☐	☐	☒	93.	When I think of the past, I tend to review accomplishments rather than brood over mistakes.
☐	☐	☒	94.	I'm either on or I'm off, hot or cold, high or low — and I don't care much for the middle.
☐	☐	☒	95.	I guard my time carefully and don't waste it.
☐	☐	☒	96.	My worries often preoccupy me.
☐	☒	☐	97.	I *savor* life as endlessly fascinating.

Strong Some None

☐ ☐ ☒ 98. I lust for more of everything — food, sex, power.

☐ ☐ ☒ 99. Why stand when you can sit? Why sit when you can lie down?

☐ ☐ ☒ 100. It's easier for me to talk about social issues than to be intimate.

Scoring: In the numbers attached to the statements, the second digit refers to that ego state in the Enneagram (e.g., 05, 15, and 35 all refer to enneagram ego state FIVE). Count the number of checks you have made for each ego state in the STRONG column. Take the highest numbered states and look at Diagram 1, Enneagram Personalities At-A-Glance. Map your numbers on the inner 3-9-6-3 triangle and on the outer 1-4-2-8-5-7-1 star. If your numbers are in a matching sequence (e.g., 4-2-8), with the highest number of checks for (2), you have probably identified your point as Enneagram TWO correctly, and the side numbers represent your stress (8) and heart points (4). More of which, later.

If, however, a number is out of sequence, you have several things to consider. There is a tendency to lean to one side or the other of your point on the *circle*. Some ELITIST FOURS, for instance, have a reclusive quality and are more like OBSERVER FIVES, while others are more production-minded and lean to the PERFORMER THREE side. These side positions are called wings. You may have several checks in one of these positions. For example, 4-1-5 may have the highest number of checks, followed by 2. Here the point is Enneagram FOUR with a strong FIVE wing.

Your checklist introduces another bit of data — your subtype. Numbers ending with a 0 show the way you tend to use your energy. Items 10, 30, and 50 refer to a survival orientation. Items 20, 40, 60, and 80 refer to a primary partnership focus, and items 70, 90, and 100 refer to a broader community focus. A later chapter, Subtypes and Sitcoms, will take these further for you, but now we want to map your position on the Enneagram circle. The next chapter uses the chart, *Enneagram Personalities At-A-Glance*, and explores the cluster of traits associated with each point.

Enneagram
Personalities At-A-Glance

A circle chart with clusters of
Enneagram character traits — examples given.

The word-clusters around each Personality Type's point on the circle name the traits and issues associated with that point. These attributes stem from decisions made in our earliest years and long forgotten. Our parents gave us both their conscious and unconscious understanding of life's opportunities and dangers. We absorbed some information in infancy. As young children we found the information reinforced by our experiences with the people who made up our family and neighborhood. We took in their messages and applied them to our life circumstances. Over time our responses settled into one of the Enneagram patterns.

The title line **Life Script Program** heads each cluster and names the pattern. For example, the Enneagram ONE program, *Perfection and Resentment,* is one in which doing things right and working hard is highly valued. It is a program we hope our car mechanic and surgeon have chosen. We honor it in technicians. We attribute it to Germans because their standards of workmanship are known. We often associate it with father-figures and oldest children, who must shape up to the adult world early in life.

Perfection justifies the behavior but is often a personal compulsion. So *perfection* is also listed as the **addiction,** a compulsive element in the personality. Alex, an engineer and problem solver, automatically sees what

ENNEAGRAM PERSONALITIES AT-A-GLANCE

9

NON-AGGRESSION/INDECISION & INDOLENCE
"I'm easy going"
LAZINESS CONFLICT
indecision **active love**
obsessive thought
Epic Tales
(Passive aggressive Personality)

8

SELF-DEFINED JUSTICE/
ARROGANCE
"I'm powerful"
LUST WEAKNESS
arrogance/vengeance
trustfulness denial
Imperatives
(Sociopath)

1

PERFECTION & RESENTMENT
"I'm right. I'm hard working"
WRATH OPEN ANGER
perfection **forbearance**
reaction formation
Preach and Teach
(Compulsive Personality)

7

EASY OPTIMISM/
UNEASY ACTIVITY
"I see the bright side"
GLUTTONY PAIN
idealism **moderation/balance**
rationalization
Anecdotes
(Narcissistic Personality)

2

HELPFULNESS &
MANIPULATION
"I'm helpful"
PRIDE OWN NEEDS
service **humility &
appropriate self-esteem**
repression
Help and Advice
(Hysteric)

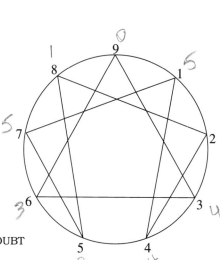

6

SECURITY/FEAR AND DOUBT
"I'm loyal"
COWARDICE/RECKLESS COURAGE
DEVIANCE
security **faith**
projection
Group Thought
(Paranoid Personality)

3

ACHIEVEMENT/
EMPHASIS ON IMAGE
"I'm successful"
DECEIT FAILURE
efficiency **hope**
identification
Self-Promotion
(Work-A-Holic)

5

KNOWLEDGE/WITHDRAWAL
"I'm perceptive"
ACQUISITIVENESS EMPTINESS
knowledge **detachment**
isolation/
compartmentalization
Dissertations
(Avoidant Personality)

4

EXCELLENCE/MOODY NOSTALGIA
"I'm unique"
ENVY COMMONPLACE
elitism **contentment**
introjection/sublimation
Sad Stories
(Depression)

TYPEFACE KEY TO DIAGRAM

Classification starts with naming. The usual designation of Enneagram points is by number and by the ego-state distortion. For our purposes, the behavior cluster descriptions in the chart are seen as Programs. That is, they are the outer evidence of a systematic way we take in information about the outer world, organize our feelings, and limit our choices of possible action.

LIFE SCRIPT PROGRAM — The Program names contain tension. The first descriptive word, in a sense, is the justification for the behavior chosen, for example, perfection or helpfulness. This quality, however, has an addictive or compulsive aspect. The second descriptive word, the negative companion of justification, holds a potent energy for change. However, it must be transformed before it can be used.

"Self-description" — A phrase which the person might use to describe his or her own behavior. For example, ONE'S "I'm hard working."

SHADOW ISSUES — The negative issue or attribute with which the person must wrestle to achieve personal integration, e.g. FOUR'S envy.

REJECTED TRANSFORMATION ELEMENT — An overlooked and avoided feeling or experience needed to complete one's personal integration. For example, when an EIGHT owns weakness, the possibility of healing comes.

addiction — A compulsion the person treats as a basic need. For example, ONE'S perfectionism.

strength needed — The particular attribute which the person gains from conscious work with the Program's problems and issues. For example, in overcoming gluttony, SEVEN attains moderation and balance.

defense mechanism — The characteristic psychological defense the person uses in times of stress (one of the forms of fight, flight, or submission). For example, TWO's self repression.

Talk Style — Recurrent forms of speech. For example, SEVEN'S Anecdotes.

(Psychological Disturbance) — The form of mental illness associated with extreme distress. For example, SIX'S paranoia.

---

is out of place or needs correction. He is invaluable in finding the "bugs" in complex telephone systems. His compulsion becomes a problem, however, when he brings it home. He observes the unwashed dishes in the sink and the sports equipment strewn over the furniture. He fumes with irritation. His awareness of what his wife and son have *not* done during the day obscures the pleasure of their lively home.

The pattern goes around the circle: the first word of each life script program names both the value sought and a distortion of it in the addiction.

Look at the word "manipulation" in program TWO, *Helpfulness and Manipulation*. A person who feels one down or in second place often chooses this program. Someone else dominates the situation, but the TWO can be supremely important to that person. The TWO can emotionally and physically support a powerful partner or boss and supply various needs. This guarantees the TWO's survival, at the least, and often considerable unacknowledged power. The power comes from *manipulation* of the other

person. This portion of the program, therefore, is closely related to the Shadow issue listed in the cluster. For the TWO, *pride of association* is the Shadow (e.g., my wife the president of the Conservation League, my boss the Senator, my daughter the writer). Think of the many jokes you have heard about possessive, controlling mothers, such as in the cartoon strip *Momma*. But the Enneagram TWO role is not restricted to women.

The phrase with quotation marks, in the cluster immediately under the Life Script Program, is a self-description the person feels comfortable to use (for example, the ONE's "I'm hard working," or the EIGHT's "I'm powerful.").

The **Shadow issue** or hidden behavior of any Enneagram pattern sounds dreadfully negative but has an interesting quality. When opened, it holds an unexpected strength. We gain the strength through struggle with our own devious aspects. The metaphor, found in folk and fairy tales, requires one to go out, find the dragon, and kill it. This is costly but gains personal freedom.

Many women have given up TWO programs, decided to meet their *own needs* — the **rejected transformation element** — and found the structure of their marriages badly shaken. (The **transformation element** is an overlooked, avoided feeling or experience needed to complete one's personal integration.) The cartoon strip *Doonesbury* touches this theme when BD leaves for the Persian Gulf and Boopsie, his beloved, joins a women's support group, learns to overhaul the motorcycle, makes her own decisions and reads the fine print in her movie contract. Her agent Sid and BD are both horrified. Neither wants a relationship with a self-sufficient woman.

We avoid the transformation element for a very good reason. It can be deadly, unless we develop the strength needed to deal with it. Consider this rejection of what we need by looking at program THREE. For the THREE, the transformation element is *failure*.

We associate the THREE program with an image of a highly successful achiever, a warrior, or a hero. It is a common male program, but both men and women can manifest it in anything that allows countable, measurable performance. Whenever our self-image is fundamental to our self-esteem, there is a temptation to enhance it at the cost of truth. Self-deceit, inflation, and *self-promotion* go hand in hand. Marketing people, advertising and real estate agents, actors, promoters, stockbrokers, businesspeople, and all the professions who want to sell their services have a place for the THREE personality.

Back to the transformation element, failure. How does this work? How does it bring the THREE to truthful self-knowledge? With failure, one's false self-assessment crashes. No more self-deceit. At first the THREE feels worthless — which is equally false but temporary, if one understands the task, for this is the dragon that we must master. Overvaluing and undervaluing are both *deception*. We can misuse either to justify choices that limit life for ourselves or other people. What we need is a better connection to our instinctive feeling responses to other people and to each specific difficulty. For example,

Burt is one of the top men in his company. When he was a small child, his father shamed him for giving in to his feelings. When he was an adolescent, his father scorned him for writing poetry. Burt grimly decided to show his father he could outdo him at the father's own game. As a businessman, he did. But he paid the same cost as his father, failure in relationship. Thirty years later, with a desirable wife, two sons in the best prep schools, and a position as head of his own section of a multinational corporation, he had proved his worth — what could go wrong?

He didn't heed the beginning. Both sons had been born while he was away on business. His wife felt deserted at crucial times when family decisions had to be made. Their competitive and fiery conflicts for a long time merely fueled the passion he felt for her. He still felt that he was a winner and had everything, even while her anger corroded her love.

As his wife's mothering responsibilities lessened, she realized her hunger for a separate life and acted on it. Burt was devastated.

That one failure was the pain-filled beginning of a long journey. He had to encounter his father and admit the shape his grudge had given to his life. He had to find the boy-poet of his adolescence, who still held his feelings. He had to forgive himself and forgive his wife as he realized the "failure" had become a gateway to finding his own wholeness again.

Addiction to success can be as deadening as any substance abuse addiction, but what the addict avoids can become the way out. Only the failure of his marriage could bring Burt to question the way he had built his life. Everything else told him he was successful. In searching for the reason he failed, he found himself.

Each element relates logically to every other element of a program cluster. For example, the *addiction* is a compulsion. The *strength needed* is an attribute gained from work on the point's problems. The *defense mechanism*, a strategy under stress, is not only a defense, but also a way of avoiding the necessary work. The specific defense does not belong solely to the person, nor is it the only one used. However, it feels particularly right and comes easily to hand. All of these elements develop from the Shadow issue. To illustrate relationship, we will look at Enneagram Program FIVE.

That's an interesting question, but I'm afraid I haven't a clue.

Isolation and compartmentalization are the FIVE's automatic defenses in times of stress. As children they learned to take the isolated position of an outside observer in order to deal with parents who were emotionally intrusive or depriving. Such children withdrew into a world of information, imaginative thought, and reflection.

Their chosen defense has a close relation to their Shadow issue — *acquisitiveness*, and to their addiction, *knowledge*. Knowledge is not wisdom. The information they acquire contains immense contradictions. In order not to be captured by data and have to deal with the discrepancies, *and* in order to continue to acquire huge hoards of information, the FIVE learns to *compartmentalize*. He tucks his data into compartments that are self-consistent — religious values in one box, economic news in another. There-after, the FIVE does not have to deal with the contradictions between

So then Howard came along. He was Canadian, but couldn't make a nest to save his soul, poor thing. But we had a lot of laughs, Howard and I. I remember one time . . .

boxes, until and when he is ready to do so. Knowledge, hoarded and not used, loses its meaning and liveliness.

The **psychological defense mechanism** works in the same way. The FIVE can continue to live in circumstances that, if he allowed himself to know the implications, would be impossible. When an individual compartmentalizes his or her feelings, separate from ethical codes and separate from economic and social data, he can make decisions that allow for personal comfort or safety but that violate human justice and the common good. When we view the homeless as "streetpeople, different from us," we shift subtly into blaming the victim and do not have to question our political part in the distribution of goods.

The **talk style,** a recurrent form of speech, is also consistent with the internal logic of each cluster. Our Enneagram pattern influences every aspect of our life. Consider the ONE's interest in finding out the rules;

ENNEAGRAM LIFE SCRIPT PROGRAMS

The **ONE** strategy is to find out the rules of the game, to master them in order to do a good job, and to win approval, if not love. The ONE wants to have a means of judging others and his or her place in relation to them.

As his **TWO** strategy, the child decides to survive through sensing what the powerful other person wants and altering himself to become or provide that want.

The **THREE** strategy is to find activities and attributes that will win the widest possible approval. The child creates his or her image with these qualities to avoid the sense of being unacceptable.

The child develops the **FOUR** strategy to prevent the immobilizing depression experienced with actual loss. Thereafter, he or she avoids total emotional involvement in any current relationship. After the real loss, the child fills his life with imagination and fantasy, explores symbolic interpretations of what happened, and plays at the edge of his desire, to be close and to be destroyed.

The **FIVE** child decides that people threaten something essential to his or her survival. She develops a protective strategy of playing possum, camouflaging her existence and reducing her needs to a minimum so she becomes as unnoticeable as possible. She then discovers she can pursue her own interests undisturbed.

The **SIX** strategy is to focus on danger, to scan the environment for all possible threats and to program his or her behavior to avoid it. An alternative is to meet danger head on and defuse it.

The choice of a **SEVEN** strategy has three elements. First, it is difficult to hit a moving target, thereby the SEVEN avoids threat. Second, a multitude of interests guarantees that no one thing or person will ever be of such importance that its loss would be devastating. Third, the interests themselves are sufficiently absorbing that no energy is left over to consider less manageable matters.

The **EIGHT** strategy is to seize control and emotional dominance. The child decides to define the game rather than be defined by it. Feeling the power to do this, the child denies her or his own vulnerability.

The **NINE** strategy starts from the self-perception of not being important enough to love. The child turns this outward. Nothing (and no one) is more important than anything else.

---

to "preach and teach" is a natural outcome. The SEVEN personality, whose special gift is easy sociability, shows it in a related gift for *anecdotes*. The EIGHT, who usually defines events in his or her own terms of power, has a natural inclination to *imperatives*. The NINE, with a lazy propensity not to edit, prefers to make a saga or *epic tale* in retelling the events of his or her life.

The final element to consider: each Enneagram type has a characteristic **psychological disturbance** or disorder. These, too, connect with the defense mechanisms. Take point SIX as an example. The defense of *projection* is common to all points because, as described earlier, we learn about our own unconscious tendencies by first shining them on other people. However, the SIX takes it to an extreme. SIXES find the real hooks other people have to hold the projection. The facts are facts, not just projected. This allows the SIX great sensitivity to details most people do not pick up. However, in situations of massive personal disorder and distress, the SIX enlarges and engrosses the outer data to a pathological extreme, *paranoia*. This goes far beyond the reality connection.

So it goes around the circle. Each cluster has an internal order and logical consistency.

The one-liner scripts, of course, do not begin to cover the complexity of an individual life. They identify only an underlying theme, often present. The author's book *Emotions and the Enneagram: Working Through Your Life Script* explains and expands the Life Scripts. In this workbook you will develop your own slant of understanding in the exercises of Chapter Four.

Exercises in
Role Play and Reversal

*Your Nine Enneagram Characters —
a warm-up exercise and a series of questions
from the point of view of each invented character.*

This Workbook section offers a process we can use to explore how emotions and feelings interact in the nine different programs known as the Enneagram Personality Types. The exercises are meditations to help us examine our own lives and to enter the mind-sets of people we believe to be quite different from ourselves. In these exercises we need to let go of our normal responses and act with the qualities of each new character.

Optional warm-up entry exercise: Sometimes we gain understanding that goes beyond words by playing with art material, clay or paint as we think. Before tackling the exercises, you may benefit from the following warm-up. After reviewing the qualities of the chart description of the point, take two felt-tip pens of different colors and doodle for two or three minutes as you feel your way into the depicted character.

Think of people you have known, read about, or watched in a film or play who match the description. Consider what you particularly appreciate about such people. Your drawings do not have to be faces or figures, just doodles! Date and label them. Later, when you look through them, you may find you have noted more than you realized.

The exercises can be done in dialogue with a partner or written directly into the book. If working with a partner, take turns. One can speak and the other can listen as you each explore for yourselves the special gift of this point, its shadow attribute, then the rejected or neglected transformation element. When you have finished, jot down a few notes or the insights may slip away.

ENNEAGRAM POINT ONE

To begin, think of a person who matches the description of Point ONE — possibly a perfectionistic boss, a reformer, a teacher — a character somewhat like the one Jack Lemmon played in the movie *The Odd Couple* — someone who's competent and virtuous but who carries a mental list of things he or she finds irritating, someone like Diane the perfectionist barmaid in *Cheers,* or the Marine in *Major Dad.* Perhaps you want a darker character. Keep that person in mind as you mull over the point-ONE qualities:

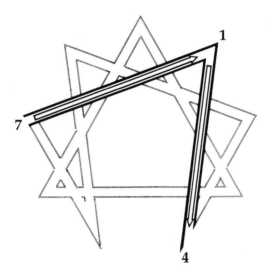

Enneagram One

Life Script: *Perfection and Resentment*
Special Gift: *A Vision of Balance and Completion*
Self-Description: *"I'm right." "I'm hard working."*
Shadow Issue: *Rage/Wrath*
Rejected Transformation Element: *Openly Expressed Anger*
Addiction: *Perfection*
Strength Needed: *Forbearance*
Defense Mechanism: *Reaction Formation*
Psychological Disturbance: *Compulsive Personality*
Talk Style: *Preach and Teach*

Point ONE has a special gift — the ability to envision the balanced, perfect running of whatever task to be dealt with, whether it's housework, a repair job, or managing the economy.

Unfortunately, he identifies his vision as of primary importance. Anyone or anything that obstructs his idea irritates him. His shadow attribute is wrath; the rejected transformation element is openly expressed anger.

Those negative emotions seem close and directly concern the vision the ONE identifies with, but they have differences. Wrath, or rage, has a scale of intensity, but it is blind. It is an out-of-control, emotionally irrational state. The body releases chemicals that allow a certain oblivion to pain. That is one reason we become addicted to rage. Chronically wrathful persons fume about and feed their rage from many sources. Actions flowing from rage are usually ineffective as change agents and, often, irrationally destructive.

Anger, on the other hand, is a normal and appropriate human feeling in response to something a person wants to have stop or change. Anger allows a focusing of rational consciousness, cutting out extraneous awareness, so *that which needs change can be known*. Openly expressing the anger can be the first step in change.

To explore these elements in your character, you need to think not only about your own feeling responses and reactions to injustice but also those of other people you have known who resemble this description. **Add whatever occurs to you. Write your notes here.**

Imagine yourself now into the character you have chosen and read the exercise as if that character were living *your* life, encountering the dilemmas you face. You can think of this as method-acting or you can view it as exploring an inner, less-known part of yourself. Get a sense of the character's body, how you would hold yourself, how you would dress, and the setting in which you would feel comfortable. Allow yourself to contact the feelings in this character's personal, private place.

As you read the questions, identify situations from your own life. Look at them from the point of view of this character. Use your first-person, present-tense voice, and write the character's response.

Your **Enneagram Point-ONE** character speaks the sentences in italics. (You might edit or rewrite these lines to make them closer to your character's speech.) You continue to write from the character's point of view, but describe events in your own life in answering the questions. **The exercise directions are given in bold typeface.**

Character speaks: *I define myself by being right, knowing the correct answer, attending to detail, and working hard. I know how things should be. Yet sometimes I think maybe I win the battle and lose the war with my work focus. I cut myself off from having fun and other pleasure. My attention to "what's wrong" rather than "what's right" takes so much of my energy.*

Think of resentments that enter sexuality. *E.g., I can do an erotic massage; my empathy with my partner's response satisfies me, but I resent it when there is no return in kind.* **Write your own version.**

Name a duty in which resentment is a difficulty for you. *E.g., I come home from having worked all day. The house is a mess. I'm expected not only to bring in money but also to shop, clean, cook, collect the laundry, and walk the dog. No one else takes this kind of responsibility.* **Write your own version.**

What would change if you openly expressed your anger and insisted the other share half the tasks? *E.g., I'm tired and cranky from doing too much. I want you to decide, right now, which tasks you will take as your share. You can do them, or pay someone else to do them, but I will not do them again.* **Write your own version.**

Is there a catastrophic fantasy lurking around? *E.g., I can't ask that of him/her. He'd leave me/beat me/go out and get drunk/use it as an excuse to . . . /never agree, and then I'd have to up the ante and leave him/her, and I don't want to . . .* **Write your own version.**

I can't swallow my irritation and I won't spit it out. I won't give up my anger. Sometimes I think rage is the only thing that sustains me. There are so many things to be angry about. The political condition of the country, the shoddy quality of everything, the poor service of sales personnel, the sheer stupidity of those who call themselves experts, other drivers on the road . . . I could give you a list into next week. **List everything that irritates you. If you run out, wait a minute and see what else comes to mind. Take as long as you need. Insert sheets/pages to this book as needed. Clean this closet of its hoard of feelings.**

The difference I see between anger and rage (wrath) is:

I expect others to shape up, but directly telling them what I am angry about is difficult. I'm uncomfortable. I can see the others don't accept, or even see, my standards of excellence. They regard me as parental and judgmental and they walk around me as if on egg shells. **Who sees a different side of you? Who has appreciated your critical mind or your sense of the superb** possibilities in a situation? Reverse roles with this person and allow him or her to say what he or she has seen and valued about you — e.g., why you have stayed friends and how the friendship might deepen. (Yes, it is a double switch.)

As I read my friend's description of me I notice that something in me wants to discount parts of it and correct or qualify other parts. How difficult it is for me to express appreciation or to accept it. **Think of someone close to you. List five things you appreciate. Have you ever told your friend what you appreciate? Why not?**

What part does jealousy play in your life? On a scale of totally proper to wildly sexual, how do you describe your sexuality? Do alcohol or drugs play a part?

How does being noncommittal work for you? What does it allow to happen — and not to happen?

What would happen to my work and my relationships if I were to substitute the idea of wholeness, completion, and inclusion instead of a never-to-be-reached standard of perfection? Imagine a circumstance in your life in which you are trying to do things perfectly. If you were to substitute the idea of completion and inclusion, what would have to change?

Would you have to give something up? What or who would you need to include?

What would you have to do before that could happen? *E.g., prior steps to get a broader picture, different values, someone else's point of view.*

There is a price to pay for change. Perhaps I might act "as if" I had acquired serenity and forbearance. **Imagine how you would like things to be in just one aspect of your life. What steps might you take toward that change? What would the price be for you?**

ENNEAGRAM POINT TWO

Imagine the character as a socially charming, helpful manipulator, or, perhaps, a nurturing mother-martyr, a flattering but self-centered giver, or a seductive pleaser. The character might be someone like the mothers played by Shirley MacLaine in *Terms of Endearment* and *Postcards from the Edge*. The TV detective Father Dowling is in many ways a male version of this type.

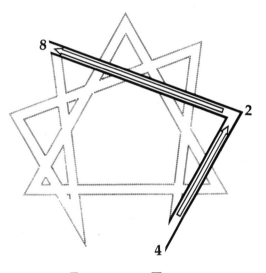

Enneagram Two

Life Script: *Helpfulness and Manipulation*
Special Gift: *Warmth and Ability to Help People to Feel comfortable.*
Self-Description: *"I'm helpful."*
Shadow Issue: *Pride of Association*
Rejected Transformation Element: *Taking Care of Own Needs*
Addiction: *Service*
Strength Needed: *Humility/Appropriate Self-Esteem*
Defense Mechanism: *Repression*
Psychological Disturbance: *Hysteric*
Talk Style: *Help and Advice*

Optional warm-up exercise: Take two colors and doodle for two or three minutes, feeling your way into this character, particularly his or her special gift for expressing warmth and making people comfortable.

If you are working with a partner, take turns in which one explores

Just remember, dear, being cute is half the battle.

while the other listens. Consider the shadow quality, PRIDE (in one's class, family, friends, or associates), and the rejected transformation element of attention to one's own needs. What do they mean in your life? **Write your notes here.**

I don't like any part of the Point TWO description. It makes me sound like a parasite, when I'm only following the Golden Rule — doing for others as I'd like them to do for me. If I'm sensitive and responsive to others' needs, why shouldn't I expect them to know what I need without having to ask or nag?

What would the world be like without mothers who give without counting the cost? Whether I'm a mother or not, I intend to be equally helpful. What would _____ *do without my help? or* _____, *who was quite ungrateful, considering I was only trying to help.* **Imagine a scene with someone close to you (marriage partner, child, parent, close friend). Think of how you value them, the pride you take in their accomplishments, and what you have contributed to this.**

What are your ambitions for them and how do you plan to bring these about?

List what you expect in return and how your partner shows awareness of what you have given. Is it sufficient? How would you like it to be different?

The TWO personality has been described as seductive but frequently frigid, with a confusion between sexual and dependency needs. These are people who need a great deal of tenderness. There is a note of exhibition in their behavior. **As you read this, what comes to mind about your own behavior when you are sexually attracted?**

When your feelings and contributions have been taken for granted or overlooked, imagine bringing this to the other's attention. How do you do it? Face-to-face, or by telling someone else who will let the offender know?

What do you tend to repress until things get too much and you explode? Do you delay confronting issues through talking around them? Do you view love as a job?

This says I need the strength *of humility. That's a laugh. What's more humble than always taking second place?* What would you feel like if the roles in your life were reversed — if you were in first place, supported by your partner?

Imagine making a marriage in which the man changes his name to take the last name of the woman's family. How would you and how would your partner feel?

What would happen to you if you lost your partner?

Well, maybe I could identify and take care of my own needs, but I want to be in a relationship. I want to matter to the person/s I love. Self-sufficiency is cold and unattractive. **What part of you once existed, perhaps in adolescence (a writer/artist/storyteller/dancer), that no longer has a place in your life? What would change if you included this part again and gave some of your energy and time to it?**

What would be the cost if it became *very* important? Perhaps you have needs no one can see unless you see them first.

ENNEAGRAM POINT THREE

Imagine the character as a successful achiever, a status-seeking competitor, a paragon of efficiency and excellence, conscious of his/her image and effect on others. Perhaps you have an older family member or someone else to serve as the model for your THREE character. It also might be someone like Oliver North of Iran-Contra notoriety; Werner Ehrhart of est; or Luther, the cocky black businessman in *Moving On Up*.

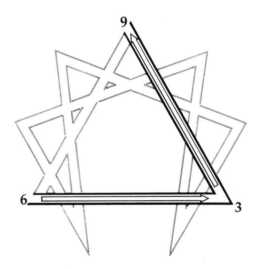

Enneagram Three

Life Script: *Achievement/Emphasis on Image*
Special Gift: *The Ability to Get Things Done*
Self-Description: *"I'm successful."*
Shadow Issue: *Deceit*
Rejected Transformation Element: *Failure*
Addiction: *Efficiency*
Strength Needed: *Hope*
Defense Mechanism: *Identification*
Psychological Disturbance: *Workaholic*
Talk Style: *Self-promotion*

Optional warm-up exercise: Take two colors and doodle for two or three minutes, feeling your way into this character, particularly his or her special gifts and ability to get things done. How important and necessary the THREE personality is in society! If you are working with a partner, take

turns in which one explores while the other listens. Consider the shadow quality, DECEIT, and the part it plays in bluffing, projecting an image, and getting things done. Then, take the rejected transformation element, FAILURE. What role has it played in your life? **Write your notes here.**

I'm the very model of American know-how and aggressive drive. I know how to compete and how to produce efficiently. I know what's wanted at work and how to provide it. I get a rush of excitement from my goals. People value what I do. Look at the outer evidence I have or am accumulating, — prestige, money, and power. I know who the people with power are. I identify with them.

Who demanded or expected you to win when you were a child? What did they want from you? What did your performance mean for them?

What did you do to excel? Was there a cost?

I know the value of image. Not only do I dress for success, I create an aura where others associate it with me. True, I have to invent *myself a bit, perhaps* market the image, *but that's part of succeeding.* **Identify one or more situations in which you have used a half-truth — or an untruth — to accomplish something.**

I don't see that as lying. For that matter, lying is as American as apple pie. Tall tales in humor and the ability to sell a refrigerator to an Eskimo are highly esteemed skills. Selling is where it is at. I sell myself with affirmations of what I know to be true or want to strengthen in myself. I don't look at the negatives if I can help it. What's wrong with that? It prevents depression over things you can't change anyway. **Who are the people most impressed with you today? Is there any cost to you in keeping up your image for them? What do you gain?**

The Enneagram THREE personality has been described as less sexual than other points, lacking empathy and more reserved. They place a low priority on relationship in contrast to their other goals. They retreat from intimacy. They seldom relax, and intimacy is difficult. **As you read this description, what occurs to you about your own sexuality?**

Look! There goes Mom!

Imagine, for a moment, the possibility of a catastrophic failure. What is the disaster that *might* happen at work, with which you wouldn't be able to cope?

What blow might fall in some other area of your life? How would you know it had happened? Who else would this affect?

What costs would you have to pay in terms of power, prestige, or money? Would there be emotional costs with friends or your partner?

I didn't like that exercise. I'm not a bleeding heart. I don't believe in indulging or showing feelings that others will take advantage of. I like to focus on the future positively, but sometimes others regard me as a workaholic. If I allow myself to fantasize a failure in personal relationship, it may devastate me. What have I lived for, just work? **Consider three failures in your life. What did you learn from each that you could have learned in no other way?**

ENNEAGRAM POINT FOUR

Imagine the hero or heroine of a romantic tragedy, Emily Bronte's Heathcliff, a melancholy artist, the southern aristocrat Ashley in *Gone With the Wind*, the gifted but moody drama queen Greta Garbo, or someone preoccupied with understanding a painful past (e.g., the character played by Meryl Streep in *Sophie's Choice*).

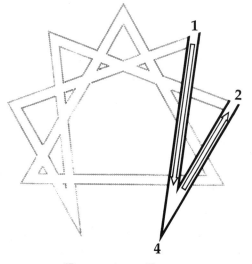

Enneagram Four

Life Script: *Excellence/Moody Nostalgia*
Special Gift: *Ability to Create Beauty*
Self-Description: *"I'm unique."*
Shadow Issue: *Envy*
Rejected Transformation Element: *The Commonplace*
Addiction: *Elitism*
Strength Needed: *Contentment*
Defense Mechanism: *Introjection/Sublimation*
Psychological Disturbance: *Depression*
Talk Style: *Sad Stories*

Optional warm-up exercise: Take two colors and doodle for two or three minutes, feeling your way into this character, particularly his or her special gift for understanding and creating beauty.

If you are working with a partner, take turns in which one explores while the other listens. Consider the shadow quality, ENVY, how and why it misuses a gift — the knowledge of a hierarchy of values. When have you

Are you sure you didn't hear a cry for help?

felt it? How did you experience it? Now, weigh the rejected element of THE COMMONPLACE — the ordinary, the opposite of specialness. How can this have a transformative role? What does it mean in your life? **Write your notes here.**

I wish I could live more comfortably with other people, but, if the cost is

lowering my standards to the ordinary and commonplace, I want none of it.
Give an example of what you consider the commonplace.

How do you create your space of beauty? In what ways does it touch
other people's lives?

Where do high standards matter most to you? When did you first
realize this — and what has happened as a consequence?

I have suffered in ways most people won't understand, but it has forged my way of looking at life, my sensitivity to beauty, and the interests that fill my life, so I wouldn't change it. Schubert once said that whenever he sat down to write a love song, he wrote about pain — but writing about pain, turned it into a love song.

Nonetheless, my preoccupation with other people's lives bothers me. I compare constantly. He or she has "more, better, or different." **Explore one connection in which another person has greater possessions, personal resources, or a partner to live the life you long for.**

The Enneagram FOUR personality has been described in women as being more envious of men, and in men as preferring unconventional sex roles. They have difficulty sustaining intimacy because they are attracted to the unavailable and less interested when the conquest is made. **As you read this description, what occurs to you about your own sexual expression?**

How does your longing work for you? motivate you to action? provide you with satisfying daydreams? Or do you avoid experiencing hope, thinking it might lead to failure? Better sad, but safe?

Imagine that you have the attribute or companion you desire now. How does your life change? How do others see you?

Five years pass. What price have you had to pay?

I'm moody and often would rather be somewhere else, alone, or with a different person than my companion. I feel hot or cold with friendships. I have difficulty feeling "in love" with anyone for any length of time. When I'm with him/her, I see all the flaws. When he/she goes away, I remember the good and how desirable that person was, but now it is too late. **Reverse roles with one person to whom you once were close. Look at yourself through his/her eyes. What do you see? What advice do you have to give?**

Imagine yourself as *contented*. What would your life look like? What do you prefer instead?

ENNEAGRAM POINT FIVE

Imagine the character as a knowledgeable hermit, an austere loner, a stingy visionary, or an isolated expert. Perhaps someone like the psychiatrist Frazier Crane in the TV sitcom, *Cheers*, the detective Detrick in *Barney Miller*, or the proper Bostonian Charles Winchester in *M*A*S*H*.

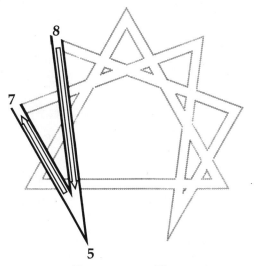

Enneagram Five

Life Script: *Knowledge/Withdrawal*
Special Gift: *Knowing "What's So."*
Self-Description: *"I'm perceptive."*
Shadow Issue: *Miserliness/Acquisition*
Rejected Transformation Element: *Emptiness*
Addiction: *Knowledge*
Strength Needed: *Detachment*
Defense Mechanism: *Compartmentalization/Isolation*
Psychological Disturbance: *Avoidant Personality*
Talk Style: *Dissertations*

Optional warm-up exercise: Take two colors and doodle for two or three minutes, feeling your way into this character, particularly his or her gift of perception, "seeing what's so."

If you are working with a partner, take turns in which one explores while the other listens. Consider the shadow quality, AVARICE — endlessly gathering knowledge or other resources, without sharing or spending them in some way for the common good. Think of what relation this has to the

feared possibility of EMPTINESS — entering a void. How might the void become a transformative element? **Write your notes here.**

I'm my own person. My solitude is extraordinarily important to me. I tolerate other people for certain amounts of time, but I don't want them to interfere with my thought and the projects that most interest me. I learned self-sufficiency early. If people need something I'll respond, but then I want them to go away. **Who frightened you when you were a child? How did they do it?**

Where did you hide? Physically? In books? In other ways?

What did you tell yourself was going on?

I live lightly. I know how to use what I've got and make it last. Some people might consider this tight or stingy, but I think of it as taking care of my needs, so I won't have to depend on anyone else. **What gift do you remember being given as a child?**

A gift is surplus, a need is not. **When and what did you need that you were not given?**

What gift do you remember *giving*? What happened to it? Do you remember how you felt?

I think I'll go type this up.

The Enneagram FIVE personality has been described as long-suffering and loyal in relationship, but utterly self-sufficient. Sexuality is somewhat muted, and there is difficulty in making the needed commitment to partnership. **As you read this description, what occurs to you about your own expression of sexuality?**

Who are the people whose respect you would most like? (These don't have to be people you know or even people living in this century.)

If you're a true FIVE, you probably have named people not known for passionate feelings. **Can you imagine a different reference group whose members have a greater intensity of emotional expression? If you tried to impress these people, how would you act?**

We have images of hanging on and letting go — a child's water wings when learning to swim, a trapeze artist's rope when swinging to catch another. Allow an image of "hanging on and letting go" come to mind. Explore it as a metaphor for your own sense of what you are hanging onto — and what might happen if you let go.

After you have thought of the catastrophe that *might* happen, let another possibility come to mind.

Imagine *feeling* detached from that which you have feared to give up. What would have to happen to allow this?

What might be a first step for you to bring this about? What is the price you are unwilling to pay?

Has anyone really seen and loved you? If not, imagine such a person. Imagine this person commenting on what is going on in your life now.

ENNEAGRAM POINT SIX

Imagine the character as an antiauthoritarian but loyal member of an institutional group, a doubt-filled devil's advocate, or a fearful procrastinator. Think of the character Woody Allen plays in his movies. Cliff and Norm, the bar stoolwarmers in *Cheers*, and Carla, the barmaid, have SIX qualities, but Carla is a feisty counterphobic SIX (see below). In her implied lifestyle, she places herself regularly in danger. The medieval poet Francois Villon had similar counterphobic SIX characteristics in his "living on the edge" lifestyle.

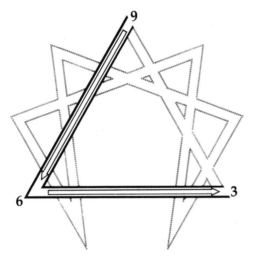

Enneagram Six

Life Script: *Security/Fear and Doubt*
Special Gift: *Care and Concern for the Group*
Self-Description: *"I'm loyal."*
Shadow Issue: *Cowardice/Reckless Courage*
Rejected Transformation Element: *Originality*
Addiction: *Security*
Strength Needed: *Faith*
Defense Mechanism: *Projection*
Psychological Disturbance: *Paranoid Personality*
Talk Style: *Group Thought*

Optional warm-up exercise: Take two colors and doodle for two or three minutes, feeling your way into this character, particularly his or her loyalty and care for the safety and protection of the group.

I don't like it here.

If you are working with a partner, take turns in which one explores while the other listens. Consider the shadow quality, COWARDICE — not taking a stand, hiding one's reservations about a popular belief. Think what relation this has to the rejected transformation element, ORIGINALITY, which feels like deviance — risking being different. How have you experienced these aspects in your own life?

Now, consider the counter-phobic (opposite) shadow quality of reckless courage driven by the edge of fear. Murphy Brown's behavior illustrates it. How have you experienced this in your life or in other people? **Write your notes here.**

I want to understand what I'm getting into. I keep my eyes and ears open for everything I may need to know. I don't want to take a chance of being caught unprepared. **When has it been particularly important for you to know what was hidden or what did not make sense? What was the cost of not knowing?**

What scene comes to mind from childhood? Who is around to protect you? Is that person capable? What qualities do you wish they had?

I don't want to rock the boat and have people upset with me. I just want respect and recognition as a worthwhile person, without having my ideas and feelings shot down. **Whose recognition do you want in your life today? Do they really see you? What would you like them to see, to understand?**

How can, or should, they know these things about you? Do you help?

What don't you like about these special people in your life? How do you convey this?

The Enneagram SIX personality has been described as having gender questions, but associating strength with masculinity and beauty with femininity. They are warm, loyal, and dutiful but fear commitment. **As you read this description, what occurs to you about your own sexuality?**

Sometimes I can't stand being at the mercy of what might happen; I go looking for trouble. **Whose courage do you admire? What advice might that person give you now?**

How *are* you different from those in your group? What might happen if you were to show it openly?

After sensing the possible catastrophe, imagine a different probability. Write your notes here.

What first step might you take to show your difference? What cost are you unwilling to pay? What do you prefer instead?

ENNEAGRAM POINT SEVEN

Imagine the character filled with easy optimism but uneasy activity, an opportunistic idealist, an intellectual generalist, an epicure like Marcel Proust, a charming dilettante, or a narcissistic escapist. Think of the protagonists in Kurt Vonnegut's picaresque novels; Sam, the ex-Red Sox pitcher now bar owner and womanizer in *Cheers*; Hawkeye, in *M*A*S*H*; Ron Harris, the Afro-American writer in *Barney Miller*; and Blanche, the outrageous flirt in her sixties of *The Golden Girls*.

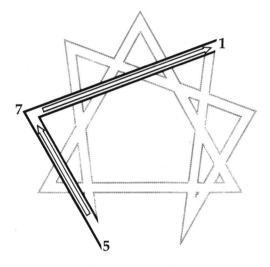

Enneagram Seven

Life Script: *Easy Optimism/Uneasy Activity*
Special Gift: *Ability to Create Pleasure and Make Things Happen*
Self-Description: *"I see the bright side."*
Shadow Issue: *Greed for Experiences of All Kinds*
Rejected Transformation Element: *Pain*
Addiction: *Idealism*
Strength Needed: *Level-headed Moderation*
Defense Mechanism: *Rationalization*
Psychological Disturbance: *Narcissistic Personality*
Talk Style: *Anecdotes*

Optional warm-up exercise: Take two colors and doodle for two or three minutes, feeling your way into this character, particularly his or her gift for making things happen and creating excitement, involvement, and pleasure.

I just got this great idea for a screen play.

If you are working with a partner, take turns in which one explores while the other listens. Consider the shadow quality, GREED — the unlimited appetite and consumption of new experiences, new possibilities, new ideas and projects, as well as choice food, clothing, and material possessions. Think of what relation this has to the rejected transformation element, PAIN (physical or mental) — that which insists on concentrating attention and refuses to allow escape. How have you experienced these elements in your life? **Write your notes here.**

I have a lot going on in my life, most of it fascinating. I like high energy people and high stimulation. Life should be pleasant. People who are overly serious and obsessed by their work or problems are uncomfortable to be around. I think it's important to make the effort needed to be charming. **How does charm work for you? When doesn't it work?**

Make a list of everything about your life that is most important. Use extra pages and sheets of paper if you have to. Mark "H" (for having) next to each item which can be consumed, used up, or owned. Mark "D" (doing) for each activity listed. Mark "R" (relationship) next to any person with whom having or doing is not the primary reason for being together. Look over your lists. What occurs to you about each of them?

What do you do about the anger of someone close to you?

With whom have *you* gotten angry? What happened? What were you afraid might happen?

The Enneagram SEVEN personality has been described as fearing intimacy and being prone to a Don Juan syndrome of many loves but no loyalty. **As you read this description, what occurs to you about your own expression of sexuality?**

Careful planning enables me to handle many different types of activity. I won't confine myself to one idea of how things should be or who I am. Commitments are the death of possibility. **What commitment is bothering you? Who wants you to make it? What would it cost?**

I like to work in spurts. Thinking about possibilities is fun; the routine demands of ordinary life are often deadly dull. **Describe the current excitement in your life. What do you see evolving? How will you feel about this project next year? when you look back on it five years from now?**

As you look at your life today, is it what you imagined it would be? What is missing?

What holds the most meaning for you? What holds the most dread? You have a gift for rationalizing. Make a case for including both meaning and dread in your life.

What causes pain in your life? Find three instances — of physical pain, emotional pain, and mental pain. What did you learn from each that you could learn in no other way?

Imagine living a moderate and balanced life in which the unanticipated might surprise you. What occurs to you? What price are you unwilling to pay? What do you prefer?

Pick one person who has cherished you but who is no longer in your life. What would this person say to you about your present quandary?

As you read these notes, what do you wish to change?

How will you begin?

ENNEAGRAM POINT EIGHT

Imagine the character as an arrogant protector, an earthy tyrant, or a vengeful, lusty lover of excess. Hard rock as well as the music of Wagner and Beethoven express this power. The setting can be that of a corporate executive or a juvenile delinquent. Henry Miller wrote from an EIGHT's point of view. John Wayne played this type of character in the movies; but think also of Scarlett O'Hara in *Gone with the Wind*, Roseanne Barr in her TV sitcom, and King David in the Bible.

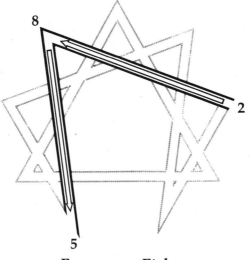

Enneagram Eight

Life Script: *Self-defined Justice/Arrogance*
Special Gift: *Care for the Underdog*
Self-Description: *"I'm powerful."*
Shadow Issue: *Lust*
Rejected Transformation Element: *Weakness*
Addiction: *Vengeance/Arrogance*
Strength Needed: *Trustfulness*
Defense Mechanism: *Denial*
Psychological Disturbance: *Sociopath*
Talk Style: *Imperatives*

Optional warm-up exercise: Take two colors and doodle for two or three minutes, feeling your way into this character, particularly the strong feeling for his or her own style of justice and the instinctual feeling for the "underdogs" he or she patronizes.

Two to one Natalie gets her way again.

If you are working with a partner, take turns in which one explores while the other listens. Consider the shadow quality, LUST — the use of others as objects or as means to a private satisfaction rather than as persons in themselves. Think what relation this has to knowing personal weakness. How might admitting vulnerability permit a transformation? What occurs to you about these aspects of your own life? **Write your notes here.**

I don't let other people intimidate me. I intend to stay on top — and they know it. **Where in your present life is it particularly important to be in charge?**

The Enneagram EIGHT personality has been described as unable to tolerate limitations and as puritanical and controlling in sexuality. The women want possession and surrender and the men want to lead. **As you read this description, what occurs to you about your own expression of sexuality?**

People generally create their own problems by being gullible, weak, or halfhearted. I fight for what I see is right and I'll take on the whole power structure, if necessary, to get my way or to prove a point. **Describe a circumstance in which you took on a high-powered adversary — or confronted a dilemma directly. (If you think you have never done so, remember a time when you wished you might have. Step into the EIGHT's shoes and**

and play it out. What might have happened as a consequence positively? negatively?)

What did you learn from this?

I enjoy provoking people to find out more about them. I like to know exactly what I'm dealing with, so I can handle my scene. If they've got what it takes, I'll respect them. I don't like phoneys. I also don't like surprises. **When have you acted this way or experienced some one else acting toward you in this way?**

How do you use space to insure your security? How do other people fit into this? What is the quid pro quo — who gets what for what?

I'm comfortable with anger, my own and others. What I don't like is indirection and manipulation. Who manipulated you in the past? What did it cost?

I trust someone who fights back, who meets me on my own ground. I don't want someone else in control of the turf. What feelings does this awaken in you now? What scene comes to mind? Can you consider how you might handle it differently? With what outcome?

What makes you feel most vulnerable?

Who can you trust to know this about you? What catastrophe do you fear if you show it to anyone else?

Can you imagine living in trust? What would have to happen or what would you have to add for this possibility?

ENNEAGRAM POINT NINE

Imagine the character as an easygoing, nonviolent protester; an indolent peacemaker; a lazy, sleeping volcano; or an indecisive, obsessive mediator. Think of Carl Jung, Ezra Pound, or TV character Henry Blake, the commanding officer in *M*A*S*H*, with his hat stuck full of fishing flies and hooks. Think of Luciano Pavorotti, or Rose, the indecisive Norwegian from Minnesota played by Betty White in *The Golden Girls*.

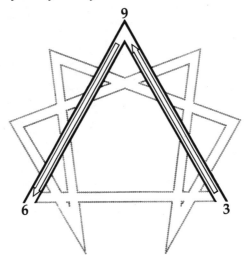

Enneagram Nine

Life Script: *Nonaggression/Indecision and Indolence*
Special Gift: *Peaceful Awareness*
Self-Description: *"I'm easygoing."*
Shadow Issue: *Laziness*
Rejected Transformation Element: *Conflict*
Addiction: *Indecision*
Strength Needed: *Active Love*
Defense Mechanism: *Obsessive Thought*
Psychological Disturbance: *Passive-Aggressive Personality*
Talk Style: *Epic Tales*

Optional warm-up exercise: Take two colors and doodle for two or three minutes, feeling your way into this character, particularly his or her gift of peaceful, wide-ranging awareness of other people.

If you are working with a partner, take turns in which one explores while the other listens. Consider the shadow quality, INDOLENCE—

You know, sometimes I almost wish you were back in real estate.

laziness, the lack of sufficient caring to insist that one thing is more important than another. Think of what relation this has to the rejected transformation possibility of entering CONFLICT. Why and how is this the cure, the way out of stuckness? How have you experienced these elements in your own life? **Write your notes here.**

I often felt completely invisible to my parents during childhood. Maybe I wasn't what they expected. I couldn't impress them, so I felt free to follow my own interests. I don't see the point of getting excited about anything. Why alienate anyone? What will happen, will happen. I don't know (or care) where time goes. Everything holds its own interest. The only thing that gets me down is having my efforts overlooked, discounted, or not credited. **Describe the last time this happened to you. What were the circumstances? What did you contribute? How did you decide to do that, rather than something else?**

I don't want other people's approval to control what I should do or be. **Does another person have a different idea of what you should do? Do you openly disagree or simply do it the way you think best? What occurs to you now about this?**

When did something similar happen to you in the past?

How did you deal with your parents when you disagreed with them? How do you bury your anger today?

The Enneagram NINE personality has been described as having few problems with gender identity other than a tendency toward indiscriminate sexuality. But relationships become routine. **As you read this description, what occurs to you about your own expression of sexuality?**

People sometimes see me as forgetting to take care of my own needs, but I seldom identify with one point of view. I see all sides of an issue; most things settle themselves. People just have to let time do it. **Who in your present life do you wish would take life easier? How would this take some pressure off you to change? How could you bring about the same result? What would the cost be?**

If you were to risk a conflict/confrontation, what might it be?

We are motivated by pain and hope. For you to act from your love, what would have to happen first? E.g., sufficient discomfort: Would you have to lose someone? Would something from the outside have to happen, an unavoidable catastrophe? Can you imagine another kind of event — someone recognizing your specialness, the unique qualities that your family never did see — to arouse sufficient hope that life might be different for you?

Who loves you? Who does not love you? What is your evidence? What would you have to *do* to feel more love? What is the price you are not willing to pay? What do you prefer, and how does it work for you?

Subtypes and Sitcoms

Only for persons fascinated by theories of personality. Those unfamiliar with Jungian Psychology should read Chapter 6 before 5.

In Enneagram theory we each have a major pattern but also access to two other sets of behavior in our heart and stress patterns. Under stress a person first uses the defenses of his or her own point. As stress increases, he moves with the arrow to behavior similar to the following point (see diagram: *Energy of the Enneagram*). For example, when strain increases, Hermit FIVE moves to a stress position of Overscheduled Planner SEVEN. In times of low tension, each person has access to characteristics of the preceding point, and the FIVE can behave from the heart position of Take-charge Leader EIGHT. These two alternative positions can be viewed as *subpersonalities*.

Yet at times we behave in ways that differ from our core personality type and its stress and heart point. How can we account for this? As children we all closely observed other family members. We are still familiar with the way their minds work and their points of view even when we do not agree with them. Their ways of seeing the world are still with us, much like costumes we can put on and act from when needed — just as we did when we played "dress-up" as children. These are *introjects*.

For example, when we discipline our children as mother once disciplined us, we may not be acting from our own Enneagram point, but from a script taken in (introjected) from mother. An easygoing NINE may

ENERGY OF THE ENNEAGRAM

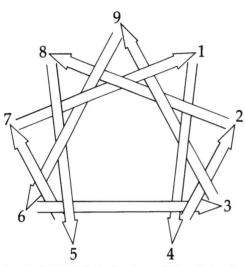

Each point connects to two other points on the circle. Under stress, a person first uses his/her own point's defenses. As stress increases, he moves with the arrow to behavior similar to the following point. In times of low tension, behavior is more expansive and can take on characteristics of the preceding point.

behave like a perfectionist ONE when it comes to her daughter keeping her room clean. This doesn't fit an Enneagram formula that says the NINE has difficulty with conflict and making decisions.

The behavior described above is what transactional analysis theory would call a parent ego state. It can also be called an introject or a subpersonality, not essential but used to accomplish some task.

We can also develop behavior called for in a role or office. Jungians speak of the persona — the image and behaviors we use in meeting the world. These usually match our Enneagram personality type, but can differ when other behavior is required by the work we do or office we hold. Dag Hammarskjold's book *Markings* revealed a mystic, not visible in his day-to-day functions as head of the United Nations. We choose our behavior, but our outer world circumstances call out much of the behavior we choose.

The Enneagram attempts to classify basic human behavior patterns. Newsmakers of the world act out their Enneagram patterns unselfconsciously and their public behavior is easily studied, but there is sometimes a hidden dimension. In contrast, the characters of ongoing television stories rarely surprise us. Sitcoms are a textbook of Enneagram-type

patterns. They have been used extensively in the earlier descriptions. Strikingly clear archetypes of human behavior fascinate us, but they also tempt us to oversimplify.

There are complications when we attempt to classify other people. NINEs tend to have a boundary problem and slip into identifying with *all* points. Performer THREEs and Overscheduled Planner SEVENs are similar in their activity level but differ in their orientation, the THREE wanting to impress some primary other person with his or her success and the SEVEN operating from a distraction strategy based in fear.

This kind of discussion may make you want to throw up your hands. It illustrates that this complex and interesting typology has the capacity to differentiate a wide variety of human personalities rather precisely, but close observation of behavior is essential.

The power of the Enneagram lies in the large number of traits it links (the clusters) and in its many dimensions. The author's book *Emotions and the Enneagram* concentrated on painful feelings that people bring to therapy. It explored the three Enneagram triads dealing with Fear (Programs FIVE, SIX, and SEVEN), Anger (Programs EIGHT, NINE, and ONE), and Depression/Sadness (Programs TWO, THREE, and FOUR) together with their connection to our common defenses of Flight, Fight, or Submission. The power of these feelings as change elements was identified. There are other dimensions that might be explored in a similar way. For example, there is the intensity and energy focus of each pattern.

Focus deals with where we aim our energy. We each tend to direct our attention and energy in one of three ways — survival, partnership satisfaction, or communal concerns. These are called *subtypes* of the Enneagram point.

The way we focus our energy differentiates one person from another within each Enneagram pattern. Identifying the three focal subtypes requires close attention to particular behavior. When a FIVE puts his energy into a communal orientation, he or she is easily seen as different from a hermit FIVE, basically concerned with survival, but may seem to function almost as an extroverted ONE. Again we must discern the underlying energy to name the subtype.

People interested in Enneagram theory have considered its relation to other typologies, for example to the Jungian classification system of introversion/extroversion, intuition/sensation, and thinking/feeling. The relationships are not equivalent. But maps are not the territory, and in psychology, theories usually supplement rather than duplicate one another. They add color and depth to the patterns.

We can find some interesting relationships using several theories to look at a specific person. Consider the chart of Jessica. Both Jungian and Enneagram personality-type classifications have been added to her subpersonality descriptions.

Jessica can play the role of any one of these characters. Consciously or not, she selects a subpersonality to accord with the scene and setting. A psychological system should not be used as an ideology. The instruments of the Enneagram, Jungian analysis, Behaviorism, and other systems do not overlap precisely. They are more like color-transparent screens layered on top of a black-and-white picture.

A good theory is coherent and consistent, but the more comprehensive it is, the better. The special gift of the Enneagram is the large number of variable traits it links and the logic of their connections.

SUBPERSONALITIES OF JESSICA

Enneagram Type	Functional Types	Roles	Attributes (Physical + Emotional + Mental + Spiritual)	Language Phrases	Origins	Triggers
SEVEN: communal subtype Persona	Extravert Feeling Sensation	Hostess Homemaker Teacher Workshop leader	Physically attractive, enjoys vivid clothes and unique jewelry, high energy, colorful, infectious enthusiasm, earthly, slightly salty tongue, humor, bright, responsive, connects people with one another, individualizes. *Wants:* Admiration, interplay, excitement with interesting people, but not intimacy or equality. *Needs:* People to care about and interact with in varied ways, to be given to, to have egocentric self-sufficiency broken	"All work and no play" is turning me into a nerd.	"Show-biz" grand-mother Family okay on massage and body care	Small groups of her public Attractive men
EIGHT: sexual subtype Shadow-introject of mother	Introvert Intuitive Feeling	Failure	Physically unattractive, lonely, hopeless beyond self-pity, mentally turned off, passive, spiritually desperate, eats too much, drinks too much, watches TV addictively, work-a-holic. *Wants:* To be taken care of, to escape from responsibilities, pain, aloneness, emptiness, sense of having failed to love. *Needs:* To be loved for what she is, not what she can do	Nothing matters because I matter to no one.	Conditional love from parents Childhood of escape routes into books linked to work-a-holic escape into other people's lives	Situation where unseen or unvalued
FIVE: survival subtype Artist	Introvert Feeling Intuition and sensation balanced	Seer Dancer Craftsman	Physically aware, particularly of textures; loses self in writing, sculpting, seeing pattern and form; not interested in doing for others but delights in products; "selfish"; feels exploited and used by Professional sub-personality; resents lack of time to develop skill; noncompetitive. *Wants:* Time and opportunity. *Needs:* Time and opportunity	See and celebrate.	Father who wrote and painted	Access to good material and creative people Experiences in art school

SUBPERSONALITIES OF JESSICA (continued)

FIVE: communal subtype Creative Animus	Extravert Intuitive Thinking	Lawyer Teacher Writer	Indifferent to physical appearance, projects high energy, enthusiasm, quick here-now intelligence, aware but impersonally involved, detached, highly principled, visionary, fascinated by interrelationship of ideas, effective in packaging and selling ideas, self-advertising, commercial, competent, very hard working, dominating. *Wants:* Power, acclaim, precision, effectiveness. *Needs:* Appropriate sphere and limitation of territorial ambitions	Life is serious. Work is all that matters. Look, it's obvious. Let me diagram it.	Surgeon father Unfulfilled ambitions and anger of mother	Almost anything
FIVE: survival subtype Daughter	Introvert Intuitive Feeling	Wife Mother Contributor to altruistic causes One who has private religious experiences Writer and teacher of ethics	Indifferent to physical appearance; accepts poverty values related to social injustice; sad, grieving, doubtful, uncertain, frightened; caring; feels tears frequently close to surface; slow thinker; mystic visionary; accepts death, failure, rebirth sequences in life; accepts searching for wisdom and meaning; passive, low energy; passionately cares about individual friendships but also has Emily Dickinson–quality of inner arrogance. *Wants:* Time to worship, express, and explore. *Needs:* Worship-prayer life, time to connect insights from other sub-personalities	My purpose in life is to know, to love, and to serve.	Mother's religious values Religious schooling including graduate studies Early nature experiences in Sierra Elitist readings and friendships	Early morning solitude Friend's letters
ONE: sexual subtype Negative Animus-introject of father	Extrovert Sensation Thinking	Wife	Physically unattractive, feels poor, will not attend to health and beauty concerns, suspicious, defiant, feels powerless, picky, constricted consciousness, tight throat, bigoted, narrow, whiny, challenging, indirectly attacking, slippery justifier. *Wants:* Revenge, recognition. *Needs:* To be given to, to have underlying values accepted	You don't appreciate me. I'll show you. Who needs you?	Relation with father	Criticism or feeling unseen

The Nine Types in Relation to Jungian Psychology

*For readers unfamiliar with Jungian Psychology
and its links to the Enneagram.*

As they begin to study the Enneagram, many people are put off by what they regard as quite negative descriptions. "Why is there so much emphasis on what's wrong rather than on what's right?" In response, some workshop leaders emphasize celebration of our different gifts. Nonetheless, the basic reason for the Enneagram's existence is to teach us to go beyond the small ego's view of what is so to a larger understanding of why we exist. This is not a small task. Information is not enough.

We are pushed and pulled into change. The degree of our discomfort pushes us to change, as does the attraction of what we hope to gain. We do not like to see uncomfortable details about ourselves. We have to reframe our difficulties to understand that they hold treasure we can claim. For example, resentment implies that one holds a vision of completion and beauty. The resentment has a meaning not yet grasped. There is a lot about ourselves we do not realize and credit.

The personality descriptions and their role-playing exercises provided Enneagram information. Some Jungian definitions and a description of the net of their relationships may help you to carry the work further.

The Life Script and other attributes in our particular cluster all belong to the *ego*. The ego is the center of the conscious personality. While we think of it simply as "I" or "myself," it includes a complex of activities. We will, we choose, and we remember. We learn to comply with the demands of our parents and of our culture in childhood. Our ego includes collective cultural and moral values plus a strategy for survival.

As our ego develops, a rift occurs within. We deal with feelings, attitudes, and thoughts that do not fit the laws and regulations around us. "Disobedience" rouses self-disgust, anxiety, and feelings of guilt, but it also mixes with the birth of self-reliance. To some extent, however, we all learn to suppress and sometimes entirely repress from our consciousness the painful conflicts of our opposing feelings and thoughts. These collect into what the Jungians call the *personal shadow*. The Shadow contains the "unacceptable" feelings, hungers, thoughts, instinctual impulses, as well as other ways of being ourselves that we have not yet discovered. (This means it also includes the rejected element of transformation.)

The *self*, the unknown center of our total personality, is also a dynamic process, a state of wholeness and inclusion. It potentially includes our conscious ego, our personal unconscious, and, like a hologram, everything of which we are or can become aware, including the element of transformation. All points of the Enneagram are part of and offer flawed windows into this profound reality.

An inner urge coming from the deeper self seems to push us to forge a unified personality. It grows stronger as we respond to our life tasks. One of the great things about the human life cycle is that if we do not get the message the first time around, the issues we must deal with turn up over and over again until we finally do.

When we begin to unify our personalities, we confront in our projections the parts we repressed. We mature when we include these thoughts and feelings in our sense of self. Integration cannot take place unless we admit these tendencies and allow them some measure of realization. How can we allow such unacceptable traits a place inside?

The *Shadow* takes a different form in each Enneagram program. It seems repugnant and unacceptable and, when alienated, can invade our behavior in evil ways. Acknowledging our dark aspect means that we are no longer unconscious of the problem and are less likely to project or deny it. We cannot get rid of it and we must deal with it. But how?

An encounter with some form of evil (pain, loss of meaning, something that appears destructive) seems to be necessary to start us on the path to consciousness. Often we struggle with a blank state of impasse. The task is to choose to endure the tension of the opposites ("I can't and yet I must"). Then some quite small shift occurs. Out of this suddenly noticeable difference comes a wider consciousness.

The personal wholeness, which comes about through overcoming a defect, requires that we go down into realities we would prefer not to know. In the process of becoming a separate and complete individual, we recognize, change, and unify our unconscious inner oppositions. We first knew these as traits of other people. We did not see them as projections of our own qualities. Like a movie projector projecting an image on a screen, we selected people to project upon. They usually had some similar peculiarity that acted as a hook, but our projection magnified it. We enlarged it to hold our own flaws. When we reown these qualities we projected, the self emerges.

Beneath the distorted visions of our small egos, we find a deeper unity. As we each become our unique selves, we realize that we have essential connections to one another. The Enneagram offers a net to gather the connections. We need openness and caring to bring its creative content over the threshold into consciousness. When we do, we *know* our humanity and the communal aspect to our identity.

As we work to realize our individual reality, we build on each other's

thoughts and insights and struggle to reach a shared and inclusive consciousness. Group therapy, Twelve-step programs, spiritual communities, spiritual directors, and other mentors can help. The commonest path to self-knowledge, however, is often not recognized as such. Partnership, particularly in marriage, is a lifetime training discipline without equal when we pursue it with commitment.

The second half of the book considers the partnership path to self-knowledge in four major phases. Then, because increasing knowledge of group systems helps our understanding of personal Enneagram transformation, a final chapter considers the relation between the individual and the collective.

PART II.
THE PARTNERSHIP PATH
TO SELF-KNOWLEDGE

Four Stages in Partnership and Marriage

*A chart of the four stages of partnership —
Individuation is like Enlightenment — Outer patterns
with partner are linked to inner "soul" events.*

No TV-watching child will accept the old line, "they fell in love, married, and lived happily ever after." Situation comedies, soaps, even comic strips build their stories from the misunderstandings of people attempting to stay close to one another.

Most of us are lively inventors of ways to relate to a person who attracts us. We play with possibilities and our responses. Our relationships go through stages of development. Most of the phases are not as easily shown as the falling-in-love or critical break-apart times. The stages parallel inner work that each of us has to do in learning to become the persons we have the potential to be. We also can become stuck personally and in the partnership.

Sometimes relationships settle into distortions of the initial phases. One couple may "act-as-if" they are a loving unit and deny any differences between them. Another couple may slip into roles that get the work of the family done, leaving the deeper, fuller reality of each partner unseen and undeveloped.

In contrast, relationships that allow both partners to live with passion and consciousness move on through an invariable sequence. No stage is skipped, although the time spent within a stage can differ from days to decades. Each stage transforms the relationship into a new form and presents specific tasks. It evolves from an earlier stage and prepares for the next change.

Understanding our own and our partner's Enneagram cluster of traits helps us to recognize the tasks and set priorities. For example, when one partner is under heavy stress, his or her entire complex of behavior shifts toward the next point on the Enneagram circle. This is not a time when ordinary problem-solving or communication skills work. First, we have to take care of the stress.

> Carl, a property developer and politician, ran into serious difficulties when the real estate market collapsed. Unable to sell several properties and unable to raise money to continue paying for them, he faced devastating foreclosures. He sensed his political credibility was also on the line. Normally a highly likable (Enneagram Seven) "bon vivant" with a dozen projects in the air, he now was functioning completely in a stress (righteous Enneagram One) mode with his wife. He could not accept or talk about her hesitation to cash out inherited stock to finance a new "venture that might save us." A solution to his financial dilemma had to be devised before he could address the partnership issue of shared decisions.

When our partner is back to ordinary point consciousness, we can talk. Questions about money, job tensions, use of time, the children, substance abuse, separate friends, in-laws, and different sexual rhythms are common among most couples. We sift them to understand the weight and intensity and what might help.

The exercises in Part I helped to identify our personality type, our partner's type, and some of the different ways in which we each view our shared world. Knowing the Enneagram, however, doesn't make our relationship problems disappear. Learning to use the information takes time.

First comes misuse. There seems to be no way around this. The patterns of information fascinate us, and we want to test them. But most of us resist being "labeled."

As students of the Enneagram, we may offer unsolicited assessments — a common misuse of diagnostic information. Like the sorcerer's apprentice, we tend to skew the details. As when a child would use a scalpel, the tool can become an inaccurate and repellent weapon. The Enneagram when used negatively is dangerous. It is worth remembering the adage: those who know, don't say; those who say, don't know.

Audrey Fain, in her doctoral study of couples using the Enneagram in their relationship (1989), identifies a sequence of stages that starts with blame. Then come stages in which each partner accepts differences and gains tolerance and appreciation. Each becomes more self-responsible, practices skill in communication, and develops shared humor.

The chart that follows identifies four major phases in the partnership path to self knowledge. The next chapters and exercises can help to expand and connect each phase to your life as you respond and also reverse roles with your partner. Each partner can increase the other's awareness of Shadow qualities and the work needed to deal with them. "Right/Wrong" games are beside the point. Neither partner has to feel blame; it is self-evident that both partners have distinct Shadow issues. Each has separate work to do, but the work touches and moves in the heart of the relationship.

THE PARTNERSHIP PATH
Part I: Outer World and

FALLING IN LOVE

A PERIOD OF PASSION, upheaval and creative energy. The beloved becomes our *projection screen*, not only that which we see but a lot more we do *not* see. In one sense, we reduce our view of the "other" to aspects and traits we desire to have. But in projecting them, these traits are not seen as our own, not developed, and not integrated. *We depend on the other remaining unknown to us in order to maintain the projection we need to grow emotionally.*

We are attracted to the positive **ENNEAGRAM POINT** and heart point characteristics of our partner.

OUTBREAK OF INSTINCTS: *Normal human behavior* is not necessarily socially acceptable.

•Aggression in wooing, chase, and capture - attempting to hook the other's projections

•Aggression from unrequited love, extreme loneliness and increased tension. Aggression in jealous fantasies.

• Sex - Conscious attitudes and ideals don't always govern our behavior. "Wild and willing" expression feels right to lovers in the moment. They feel child-like and out-of-control.

SPIRITUALLY AND MENTALLY ALIVE: Joy in feeling fresh responses to old sights and events, and in openness to new ideas. The "other" is imbued with mystery. This delicious state of knowing and not knowing self and partner, by its nature can not last, but in it we glimpse a possibility of wholeness that later we will long to recapture.

ADAPTATION TO POWER ROLES

A WORKING PARTNERSHIP begins in home, children and community. Personal relations shift as we create rules, roles and expectations which order the relationship. Stress enters from the Economy, job and other persons.

With the first *suppression of oneself for fear of losing the partner,* a power adaptation begins, mirroring adaptations made to authority figures. Then, in ways similar to children, we rebel and conform to what the other expects. Liveliness and compatibility reduce as we *structure our lives to match our decade's spirit and style.* Although productive and satisfied in most ways, we feel less zest.

WE OPERATE FROM THE DEFENSES OF OUR RESPECTIVE ENNEAGRAM POINTS, forgetting who we are and what our shared vision of life has been. This type of working partnership characterizes most marriages much of the time and can last indefinitely, unless a crisis erupts.

TO SELF KNOWLEDGE
Relationship to Partner

DARKENING CONFLICT

When the **"other"** (inner or outer) **demands to be seen,** Dissonance! Sex is inhibited and unenthusiastic; projections bring family incest taboos, i.e. we don't *want* a child or a parent type mate.

We suffer under the weight of a heavily regulated relationship without illusion that formality and conviviality = intimacy. We are depressed, angry, and hurt with fantasies of separation. We have lost self-esteem. We long to ESCAPE! -throw out, be rid of the monster, or bore we used to love. We are disappointed - and *in a hurry!*

Positive aspects of life are projected onto outer world, new career, new infatuation or religious conversion.

USE OF ENNEAGRAM STRESS POINT BEHAVIORS.

TYPES OF RESPONSE TO PARTNER:

1. We can refuse to recognize and deal with differences; repress data and our reaction to it. Later, we will probably repeat the problem with another partner.

2. We may try to control partner by anger, disapproval, withdrawal, or pouting.

3. We experiment with separation. *Goal of SEPARATION, whether acted outwardly, or only inwardly, is to REMEMBER SELF and achieve consciousness and passion.*

4. Uneasy and ambivalent, we begin true work to integrate Shadow. Too much attention has been paid to how life should be; who we and our partner should be; not enough attention to who we and our partner are.

REMEMBERING SELF AND COMPLETION IN UNION

Our capacity to reflect can develop an **inner vision not distorted by prejudices** (personal or collective). We recognize the image of ourself as victim and the other as persecutor is a distortion.

In **REMEMBERING,** we connect our present marital problem with the rest of our life, WHO WE ARE AND ARE BECOMING - WHO WE HAVE BEEN AND WHERE WE COME FROM. We find the limits of our personality and the possibilities. We often can find a way out of the painful situation and come to a different relationship with the same spouse.

We learn the use of the **ENNEAGRAM'S REJECTED ELEMENT** after examining how our partner has held this element for us. We move through detachment to observation to understanding, then from understanding to here and now simplicity.

For our own completion, wholeness, and health, we need relationship. We need to become who we are - and to *suffer the natural pain that results from what we are.*

Love is a deeply devoted commitment, based in reality. The well-being of our beloved is essential to our own. The goal of our inner work is passion and consciousness. Through compassion with our partner, we renew affection.

FORGIVENESS: We confront our own Shadow power drive and competitiveness. We learn to forgive our partner, our parents and ourselves.

THE PARTNERSHIP PATH
Part II: Inner World and Relationship

FALLING IN LOVE

PRE-STATE: Stagnation with little conscious awareness. The Psyche rebels against a narrow ego which is out of touch with SELF, then, *one falls-in-love.*
•Dormant parts of our personality and creative energies awaken.
• Our contra-sexual (Anima/Animus) aspects are projected onto the other person.
• Our Persona brightens and is pro-tected/contained by an archetypal SELF connection.
• Our Ego is *full of one's self,* self-confident, energetic.
The Psyche becomes active, receptive, spiritual and soulful through infatuation. Projection is necessary so that these inner qualities can be known. The floodgates from the Unconscious are opened. Sex, senses, trust and energy are all experienced differently.

ADAPTATION TO POWER ROLES

INTERPLAY BETWEEN EGO, ANIMA/ANIMUS, AND SHADOW: We repress traits or feelings through defense mechanisms to divert attention away fom unacceptable traits, urges, feelings, memo-ries, and fantasies - positive & negative.

Easiest way for conflict to be diffused is to remain unconscious.

When we stabilize relationships, we **identify with collective images** - Everyman/Everywoman. We ignore differences.
Symptom of a larger difficulty: repression and adaptation away from life-filled personal spirit.
Shadow contents are projected onto the Partner, whom we also endow with the *authority of the collective,* an image which constrains us and limits our expression.

TO SELF KNOWLEDGE
to the Unknown Parts of Oneself

DARKENING CONFLICT

CHAOS OF INNER STRUGGLE:
Pain prevents Ego from recreating equilibrium, but all other psychic elements push and pull. The Shadow and negative Anima/Animus projections onto the partner deepen. Floods of Shadow feelings and perceptions about power, betrayal, and abandonment are projected onto partner. Positive aspects of life are projected onto the outer world or a fascination with a new career, a new infatuation, or a religious conversion.

CHANGE: depends entirely on our conscious involvement in our own drama, the decision to focus on our own need to change, while suffering our longing for a deeper relationship and longing for a more instinctual expression of sex and aggression.

Time in this phase can last from days to years.

REMEMBERING SELF AND COMPLETION IN UNION

REMEMBERING: We accept and integrate parts of ourselves that personally and culturally we have not wanted to know and see.

As we disengage from our Shadow process, the **ENNEAGRAM** script lightens and the specific Point strength is attained.

Pain is the impetus to self-knowledge.

Step by step we encounter our own Shadow, our own negative Anima/Animus and our use of our times and culture. Memories inform us, not only of the pain done to us, but also of the pain we have created. In avoiding our own pain, we have inflicted pain on others, especially on those closest to us.

Re-Owning the positive Anima/Animus ultimately brings the Psyche back to relationship and to SELF, not solely in reaction to partner.

It introduces the Ego to new parts of the personality.

Instincts, aggression and sexuality are integrated as parts of the SELF.

8

Falling In Love

*Passion, upheaval, creative spiritual and
mental liveliness, difficult-to-accept instincts,
projection of everything desirable onto partner.*

The experience of "falling in love" is central to romance. To some extent it is also needed in all major commitments. We fall in love in order to know who we are. "Tepid" doesn't work in attraction to our partners, our babies, our professions, or to our spiritual/religious path.

We long to merge our lives. We want to become one and to feel passionately attached to our lover. While in this state we feel unfamiliar, sharper body sensations. Our skin feels every touch. We observe details unseen before. We hear more. Our energy pours out. Time drifts or stands still, depending on whether we are together or apart. Strange feelings and desires to act aggressively or masochistically can startle us. We fear losing one another. When we are apart, we feel lonely and incomplete.

Wild mood swings with insecure, obsessive, adolescent, out-of-control thoughts and feelings become familiar. Our similarities with our partner stun us; we overlook our differences. We imbue our partner with mystery. Our lover becomes our *projection screen*, not only that which we see, but a lot more that we do *not* see. In one sense, we reduce our view of each other to aspects and traits we desire.

In projecting the traits, we cannot own, develop, and integrate them as ours, but we become conscious of and value them in our partner. *We depend on our partner being partially unknown. It allows us to develop the projections we need to grow up emotionally.*

Meanwhile, we easily give and take. We do not expect our lover to change to please us. Our excitement, perceptions, and stimulation are high. Neither of us wants to appear insensitive or selfish. A childlike part has reawakened a flow of inner and outer possibilities in each of us. We feel more alive. We see and value our own qualities from our lover's eyes. We may also notice that we are highly attractive to everyone else during this period. We have the "start-up" energy to make a commitment and change our life circumstances. Everything seems to be going our way.

We do not understand how this has happened and we often confuse falling-in-love with love. Each is an indescribable phenomenon we can know only through experience. John Destein, in *Coming Together, Coming Apart*, describes the major difference,

> Infatuation is a finite period of passion and the awakening of dormant parts of one's personality, whereas love is a reality-oriented commitment and deep-rooted devotion . . . in the former we love our projections on the other person, while in the latter we love the person on whom we have projected.

Infatuation can grow into love or it can be a temporary flare-up of passion that passes. Sexual feelings deeper than any we may have experienced before run from ecstasy to agony. We even accept pain as part of the joy of being alive.

Sexual attitudes, desires, tendencies, and behaviors are but one aspect of our need for love and union, but they dominate this period. Whether we like it or not, sexuality enters our consciousness in fundamental oppositions: possession/loss; virgin/whore; protector/satyr. When we fall in love, we move into this dark instinctive territory.

Normal human behavior is not necessarily socially acceptable. "Wild and willing" sex, childlike and out-of-control, feels right to lovers. It does not always fit the way we prefer to think of ourselves. We can become quite aggressive in the chase and capture of our loved one's attention. We also can behave aggressively while suffering from loneliness, tension, and jealous fantasies if the one we love does not love us. All true feelings — hurt, sadness, disappointment, and joy connect us to a person and a setting. The

feelings have purpose. They provide us with information about our emotional responses to certain events and conflicts.

We share with everyone our need for relationship, sexuality, and aggression. We live in a peculiar time in our culture — a culture that emphasizes material possessions and consumption. Our needs are exploited commercially. Television and other media link our relationship goals with material goods. In addition, marketing people saturate their commercial messages with sexual signals and "entertainment" violence in order to compete with one another for our attention. Our awareness flags, our responses deaden and the ante goes up — more sex, more violence, more action. Some of us hardly notice the cost — less talk, less thought, less feeling, less caring, less attention to the subtle interplay of attraction. There is also less sense of community, less personal and civic action, and less sense of our oneness.

What a gift falling-in-love is to awaken our curiosity again, our instincts and feelings, our spirit and intellect, in a natural way.

While we are in love we talk more, with greater depth and caring about our life and ambitions. Our feelings prompt us to closeness. Our talk binds us into each other's history. We share our tragedies and triumphs; admit our faults; analyze our desires and tastes, our friends and families. Everything takes on greater meaning as the process brings each of us into the other's world. Comradeship deepens with this one person who sees us clearly and cares.

Even as we build the relationship, we sometimes doubt that it can last. Do we have a right to such happiness, to passion and fulfillment? This delicious state of knowing and not knowing self and partner, by its nature, cannot last, but in it we glimpse a possibility of wholeness that later we will long to recapture. Each partner sees in the other person possibilities not yet born. Each relishes the other's qualities with generosity, and without competition.

In reading the description of falling in love, what most touched your own experience?

EARLY HARMONY   M.K. Brown

List all the people you have loved; all the projects and enthusiasms with which you have "fallen in love." What do they have in common? Which stand out in your mind? We often choose people to love who have traits similar to our parents. What occurs to you about your list? about the men on it? about the women on it?

What is your Enneagram type? What was/is your lover's? Do you share a point or a wing? What qualities do you have in common? What Enneagram type was your parent of the same sex as your partner? What qualities do they have in common?

Review your Enneagram traits and heart-point qualities and note how these became active projections onto another during your childhood or adolescence. *E.g., As a preadolescent Enneagram FIVE, I was busy reading my way through the library, A to Z. I had finished Zane Grey and was well into the H's with Richard Halliburton when I discovered LOVE. I didn't know about boyfriends, but I already knew my addiction to knowledge. My boyfriend, when I got one, would have to be smart.*

Bill, an overweight, myopic, high school freshman with acne scars, was reading De Joinville's Chronicles of the Crusades *that summer. I had a large vocabulary of words I had not heard pronounced. Bill arrogantly corrected me on "abysmal," and I was in love! I can smell the campfire, see the sparking flames, and hear the summer dance band in back of us ("Lavender blue -oo, dilly dilly, lavender gold . . ."). Despite the surging, melting feelings in my body for this "strong, silent, and stern leader of men," I had no social skills to attract his further attention. I learned he meditated Zen-style. In the forties, among Jesuit-trained schoolboys, that was not avant-garde but merely weird. For me, it was a hook that could hold my ideals. The real hook was Bill's similarity* to my father in his valuing of knowledge, uncontaminated by emotions. **Write your own version.**

Describe the qualities and traits of your first love. Put "I am . . ." or "I have . . ." before the qualities that attracted you. How do they fit?

What has happened to these qualities in your present life?

Sometimes the first love, but more often the "great love, now over," serves as a screen, contaminating a current relationship. "What might have been" is still a latent fantasy and ready to begin again. A Jungian term for this is *the ghostly lover.* You can dissipate it by recognizing positive qualities of your own that you projected onto the ghostly lover.

First, list the qualities (positive and negative) of your opposite-sex parent — or an opposite-sex favorite relative from your childhood. Then list the qualities of your partner and one or two lovers (or loved) from your past. For example,

> Father: Responsible, capable, strong and attractive, knew everything about everything, "stolid but solid."
>
> Uncle: Playful humor, showed us how to draw, liked children and played rowdily with us. "Black Irish," with blue eyes and slight build. He was called "Irresponsible."
>
> First love: Humor, artistic talent, wide interests, playful, independent, appreciated me without taking me too seriously, tall, dark, and handsome. Uninterested in marriage.
>
> Later love: Humor, knowledge and academic achievements, imagination, good-looking until he shaved his beard.

List your own examples. Be as specific as possible. The particular physical details can give you clues about projection hooks.

You might now try the same exercise with the qualities of your same-sex parent.

Look through the list. Underline or use a highlight pen to mark the qualities you have or might claim and develop as your own. A term for the image of the opposite sex that you carry around inside you is the *anima* (feminine side of the man) or *animus* (masculine side of the woman). **What occurs to you about the range of qualities you've listed?** *E.g., Responsible/irresponsible is still an internal question for me.*

Imagine yourself as the person who has the positive qualities. Claim them. Now return to yourself and jot down some adjectives. What are you like? *E.g., laugh and sparkle, quick thought and easy humor, kinder, less critical, attentive, loving, softer, look better, life is lighter.* Write your own list.

How do other people experience you? *E.g. , prolific, creative, intelligent, and funny.* **Write your own list.**

When you were in love, what surprised you about your own aggression? about your sexuality? your humor? your intellect? your spirituality? What would you particularly like to recapture from that period in your life?

Why might you *not* want to re-enter that period?

Role Adaptations

Partnership works but self-suppression rules —
then Enneagram behavior pushes us to conform or rebel.

A critical incident changes our "in-love" state. It begins the very first time one of us accedes to our lover's wish while suppressing our own out of fear that we may lose the partner or the partner's high regard. We sense we have to compromise our spontaneity, inhibit or repress some aspect of ourselves in order to hold onto our lover. This response is familiar. Earlier in our lives we felt less certain about our worth. Our reaction now, as it was then, is made out of fear *of rejection and abandonment*. It mirrors adaptations we made to parents, teachers, and other authority figures in our lives.

We begin to modify ourselves. In the exercise section we will explore five arenas of conflict — money, decision-control, sex and affection, children, and substance abuse — in which these compromises take place.

The routines and roles we work out are tepidly satisfying and get the work done, but something is missing. Perhaps we forget it. Perhaps we put the awareness away as a childish unrealistic longing. Our Enneagram state of ordinary consciousness again prevails. Our expectations of one another *order the relationship*, as we create structures and a lifestyle matching our decade's spirit. For example, the spirit of the sixties included sexual mores that were promiscuous by the standards of the fifties. Some partners initially acting in the spirit of their time found conflicts surfaced between them with the birth of children. They did "adjust." But still, the compromises infected and reduced their liveliness and sense of compatibility.

We focus our aggression with each other on maintaining the rules of the structure. Then we act out like children rebelling and conforming to what is expected. We treat our partner as our parent in this respect. We no longer relate primarily to each other out of compassion for the other's need.

Our differences emerge. We view our lover more objectively, somewhat like a business partner. We begin to think that we don't want to spend quite so much time together. We come out from what felt almost symbiotic while we were in love and re-establish our own boundaries. We become aware of subtle differences in our thoughts and often spend more time talking about opposite sides of an issue. For some of us, these differences can be a source of challenge, for others they are a disillusionment.

In this period, each of us has activities and relationships apart from the other. Each redirects attention to the outer world. Personal interests often seem more important than developing the relationship. Self-esteem comes from the exercise of power rather than the partner's regard. Conflicts over decisions, money, activities, or children are somewhat routine.

We need some way to resolve these conflicts if we are to maintain our emotional connection. Each of us has a well-defined identity in our family, work, and community roles. But habit creeps in like sleep. We operate from the defenses of our Enneagram point, forgetting the vision we once shared and what our reactions were in the first phase.

What do you remember of the first suppression of an aspect of yourself for fear of losing your partner (fear of rejection and abandonment)? *E.g., I don't recall the first time, but generally I avoid friends and activities that will bore him.* **Write your own version.**

Better a little shy than always running off at the mouth, I always say.

When you are in stress, to what Enneagram position do you move? What position does your partner take in stress? How do these relate?

Examine your Enneagram point defenses and your Shadow issue. When did these become active with your partner? How do they interplay with his defenses and Shadow issue? *E.g., As a Seven, I rationalize my overcommitted schedule and gluttony for "adventures." The plain truth is that routine bores me. When [my partner], a ONE, has booked us for an evening* with her orthodox family, I want out and can invent reasons not to be there. She resents my freedom, becomes more rigid, and seldom wants to play anymore. **Write your own version.**

Do the following exercises for yourself, then reverse roles with your partner. Think about your parents as Enneagram personalities. What were their conflicts during your childhood? How do these relate to your difficulties with child-rearing and other mutual goals?

It has been said that the misuse of our sexual energy and our self-deception in regard to it is the primary cause of our being stuck, our refusal to wake. What occurs to you about your partner as you read this? about yourself?

Money provides an amazing symbolic system to express the problems of value, of being valued and of valuing. It is measurable and easier to talk about than the feelings that surround its use. **If you are working with your partner on this material, you might each take out the small change you carry and count it, then without words, give as much or as little to your partner as you wish *at this moment*. That done, notice how you feel and what thoughts or images come to mind, without yet commenting.**

Again count the amount. Now take from your partner's pile, whatever amount you wish.

Now you can discuss your feelings as well as other considerations — equality, fairness, sharing, punishing, rewarding. Think about how your parents handled money and which parent you most closely resemble.

How have you taken in your parent's money conflicts?

We link money with power and, therefore, control. Money often substitutes for love or acceptance. Many people assess their self-worth by comparing how much they make with how much others earn. This conditions an attitude that gives less value to mothering and to household and volunteer tasks than to paid work. A student in her late thirties describes her position: "As a nonwage-earning housewife, I feel my mothering and household management is not equally valued, even though it would cost to hire someone to do it. I haven't made it in the real world."

What a deadly cultural infection that insists on seeing everything, everyone, in terms of money. **How has this money screen entered your partnership?**

Marriage has a fundamental economic base. Much household time is taken up with practicalities that involve money — shopping, paying bills, preparing meals, tasks that keep the household running. Today households are not being run well for many reasons. In a time of recession, there is less money to manage on. The vast majority of married women work outside the home, and this means less time is given by both partners to closely managing money and household tasks.

Our economy pushes people to buy more than they need. Few of us wait until we can pay cash. What seems more important is a regular monthly payment setup with no real question about the total cost, comparative interest rates, or real need. **How do you divide money decisions in your partnership? What does this division imply? How do you experience your Enneagram Shadow issues in relation to money?**

We have become a society of people constantly in debt and always wanting more. Blaming the partner for not providing his or her share of the needed income obscures basic issues that are societal and cultural. We need to overcome our individualism and act within groups in a social and political way to change these facts. Attitudes toward money come from many sources — "the way it was done at home," "the kind of person I like to think of myself as," reactions to fear, competition, and insecurity. All play their role.

It is not easy to talk about money. A money economy can promote a compulsion to work that subordinates man to things. Issues of greed and competition arise together with envy, resentment, aggression, and possessiveness. How the partners handle these matters define the family values and the Enneagram-type conflicts.

There are nonmonetary costs to earning money. These are primarily the quality of life and of family relationships. Desire for money can take the place of other genuine human needs. We can place too much emphasis on an industrious, economically rational approach to life, or, ostrichlike, we can refuse to get involved with planning.

Reverse roles with your partner. Explore the question "Why am I working and for what?"

What is it about *you* that you would like your partner to see and understand? What do you suppress in order to preserve peace? When and how don't you feel seen? *E.g., She's so practical. I need to have a dream, something to plan, play with, imagine, and look forward to bringing alive. I suppress my playfulness. Home is nothing but work.* **Write your own version.**

What is it that you are depending on your partner to do? to gain something in your life you would not otherwise have? *E.g., I want her to manage our social life, to have friends in for dinner, to entertain. It would help* *me to have more business contacts. I don't make friends easily. She should provide the bridge.* **Write your version.**

Does your Enneagram point of avoidance play a part in this? *E.g., the THREE, who in avoiding "failure," does not risk doing anything new where he or she feels no special competence.*

How do you deal with your own anger? your aggression? your partner's anger? your partner's aggression?

How do you each use food, alcohol, or another substance to make a nonverbal statement to the other? When? What are you assuming? How might you check this out?

How do you experience your own sexuality? How are you dealing with your partner's? How do you limit each other? What secret "conditions" may be operating? *E.g., If you would only, . . . then I would . . . or I won't let myself go/enjoy you until/unless you . . .*

The chief obstacle to sexual pleasure is fear — fear of being hurt, fear of being wrong, fear of being ridiculed, an almost endless list. Risking vulnerability once drew you together. When couples encounter their first conflicts, they often start to risk less and interact with deadened feelings. Just as they once did with parents, they find it easier to hide behind defensive barriers.

List the rules of your partnership, explicit and implicit. What is the difference? What implicit demand are you making or would you like to make to have the other change? In doing so, how are you limiting yourself? *E.g., Each of us has to contribute equally to household expenses and equally to household work,* may be the explicit rule. One partner may implicitly assume another clause, *Until we have a baby or I enter law school, then we'll . . .*

How do you know when your partner is in stress? What Enneagram behavior is the strong signal? What do you do? When do you recognize that *you* are in stress? What do you do when both of you are in stress?

Do you support one another in dealing with your children? Are your messages clear? Are they given in such a way that they preserve the child's and also the partner's self respect? If there are stepchildren, do you both share the parenting, or is there a mine/yours exclusion? What does this imply? Are you willing to check this out explicitly with your partner? with the child?

How do you tolerate ideas and feelings from your children that differ from your own? How do you decide who owns the problem (e.g., that it is a matter for the child to decide or a family matter)?

Darkening Conflict

The suppressed demands to be seen — dissonance!
Separation, inner or outer, to regain consciousness
and passion — Enneagram stress-point behavior.

The third stage in partnership also begins with a single decisive event. An inner protest erupts. TOO MUCH — this has to change — my wishes count — I must be seen!

Unless we let ourselves know and act on our increasing discomfort with the adaptations we have made, unless we are willing to identify our inner conflict, we enter a half-alive state. We know a sense of emptiness, and worse terrors loom if we wake. We may try to convince ourselves it is better to stay asleep, but something inside will not accept that.

The third stage therefore involves a darkening conflict with our partner, which grows in widening circles to include our professional compromises, unproductive religious routines, and other matters we used to take for granted. As with the time of role stagnation, this period, too, can last days, years, or decades.

> Carl, the (Enneagram SEVEN) real-estate broker mentioned earlier, had to work out his business problems before he could tackle the relationship issues. Then, however, things got worse before they got better. He experienced his wife's financial questions as attacks on his judgment. Her growing freedom to think her own thoughts and voice them threatened the status quo.

Sometimes the transition to greater independence between partners is unacceptable to one or both. We do not want to go forward but back. We can hunger for the engulfing closeness that gave us a sense of identity, power, and meaning. We want to look for it with another partner if we cannot get it from the first.

Our unfinished issues from childhood color and seep through our present life. If we did not deal well with our adolescent task of separating from our parents, it may distort how we see our partner — "this person who wants to run my life." We ignore our own role. We reject and avoid our Enneagram element of transformation. A hostile-dependent bond of anger and conflict can tie us together. We will use endless rounds of mutually-inflicted pain to prove that we are victims, betrayed, let down, and wronged.

Another way of looking at this is that we choose a partner with whom we experience trust and safety. Then very gradually over time we test one another by showing the sad, angry, difficult, and wounded child that we all carry around inside. Secretly and usually unconsciously, we hope that our partner will deal differently with this part that we have been unable to heal.

Often, however, our partner, no longer in the ideal lover/parent role, brings his or her own wounded child to the encounter instead. Neither can help the other while each holds onto the needy part. The partner's lack of response then feels quite like the part of our parent that did not see us and rejected our need originally. That lack of response becomes the projection hook. For example,

> Martha, a hard-working attorney, married Ed, an easygoing writer who kept his own hours and, after long years of bachelorhood, was indifferent to housework and repair. Initially she loved his sensuality and Enneagram NINE peaceful lack of tension. Whenever her work schedule heated up, however, she resented his "lack of discipline." She noticed that he never seemed to finish anything. He was careless about details. She felt he did not love her.
>
> Ed, in turn, began to feel that whatever he did, she discounted. He said she was aware only of his failings. Preoccupied with her work, she did not even greet him on the days she prepared to go to court.

While exploring their impasse in psychodrama, they found that each had experienced similar feelings in their adolescence. She had felt unacceptable to her father for reasons she could not imagine, while her younger brothers could do no wrong — and did no work. She studied, performed, and worked as hard as her father did. Nothing served to win attention. So she worked her Enneagram THREE program harder and got some grudging approval. It became her lifestyle until she fell in love with Ed. But now — he seemed to act like her brothers, and not to see *her* any more than her father had.

Ed remembered feeling unseen by his demanding, accomplished mother when he was an adolescent. He would run away at night, hitchhike with truckers, and return exhausted before dawn. He often slept through classes. His mother did not notice that he was gone. Her only concern seemed to be that his grades did not measure up to his older brothers.

Martha and Ed had managed to recreate with each other the painful conditions they had each experienced with their own parents in childhood. Each of them could pinpoint a specific age for the child part that appeared during their conflicts. Taking care of and reassuring these "inner children" had to be a part of their marital journey.

When Martha could let herself feel Ed's love for her and also her self-esteem, she could make clearer agreements with him. As an Enneagram NINE, Ed needed to risk open conflict to spell out to her that leisure was a basic need for his creativity, which he would insist be included.

In relationships that push toward growth, the inevitable period of darkening conflict is difficult. The process of projection, in which contents from the negative side of consciousness are thrown out and hurled at the partner (whether aloud or inwardly), is one of our most uncomfortable ways of learning.

Carl had experienced a father who had abandoned his mother and himself — at least that was the way his mother presented the story. His mother did not seem to regard men too highly, including Carl. His victories were not celebrated. He was the target of a stream of criticism throughout his adolescence. Home was a place to stay away from.

When his business became difficult, home felt much like it had in his childhood. His wife's questions felt like his mother's criticisms. She seemed equally disinclined to celebrate his victories.

Carl's task was to separate his wife, who genuinely loved him, from the negative mother projection he placed on her. It was not easy. His wife had hooks to hold the projection. With a perfectionist, intellectually critical, Enneagram One personality, she did have ideas and values that differed from his.

However, she loved his extroverted, flamboyant nature, so different from her own. He gave her pleasure, even while his actions worried her. She had to learn to mention the positive qualities she valued: ONES do not find stroking or praise an easy thing to do. He could then begin to hear some of her reservations as such, rather than condemnation.

In the earlier period of infatuation, projection also operated. It was easier to deal with when we experienced positive qualities in each other. What we are aware of we encourage to develop. Sadly, the same holds true for the negative projections. Partners learn each other's points of vulnerability. We know how to hurt back when we are attacked. Just as a government can prefer military solutions to negotiated settlements, we can prefer our favorite psychological defenses over compromise and negotiation. Our strategic defenses then form an impenetrable barrier to the intimacy we long for. Sex becomes inhibited and unenthusiastic. Our projections bring family incest taboos, i.e. we do not *want* either a child or a parent-type mate.

We suffer under the weight of our heavily regulated relationship without the illusion that we have intimacy, even when it works in the outer world and is congenial. We feel depressed, angry, and hurt. We fantasize about separating. We long to *escape* — to throw out, to rid ourselves of the monster or bore we used to love. We are disappointed *and in a hurry!*

We now project onto the outer world the positive aspects of our life — a new career, a new infatuation, or a religious conversion.

The task is to learn that *we* are the enemy; to learn that much of what we experience as coming from the partner is a mirror of our own unowned aspects. It is emerging from our own unconscious and needs to be known. We have to discriminate between what belongs to us and what to our partner.

It is not easy. We can hold on to our true perception that our partner has one searingly obvious fault, against which our own flaws are minor. We can use this as an excuse not to do the self-examination we need.

> For several years, Carl tended to escape from home, even as he had in childhood. Business trips, extended vacations in the mountains with boyhood friends, expensive (new toys) cars, vacation hideaways. Why, he asked, couldn't his wife see these as "investments"? She did not appreciate him. He could point to his obvious financial success and trust his obvious good judgment. She was wrong in her judgment about financial matters and about him.

We usually try a sequence of moves. In the earlier phase, we refuse to recognize and deal with our differences. We repress data and our reaction to facts. If we continue this now, we will exit the marriage and probably repeat the problem later with another partner. We may try to control our partner by anger, disapproval, withdrawal, or pouting — a deadly dead-end.

We next experiment with separation. *The goal of separation, whether acted outwardly or only inwardly, is to remember self and to achieve consciousness and passion.* However, we do not know this consciously.

Finally, feeling uneasy and ambivalent, we begin our true work to integrate our Shadow qualities. We have paid too much attention to how life should be and who we and our partner should be, and not enough attention to who we and our spouse are.

> Carl finally felt the pain he had avoided all his life and it became his means for transformation. He reached a point where he felt he had to separate from this negative, unappreciative woman. He told her so, expecting this would be a relief to both of them. Her genuine upset and her willingness to consider what she had contributed to his pain astonished him.
>
> Now he had to question whether he was carrying hurts from his childhood into the relationship. His real work started and took several years. He took another look at what his mother had said and been. He searched for his father and found him. The father was not a perfect man, but he hadn't willingly abandoned Carl.
>
> Carl had to know and express his anger toward his mother. Then he found the pain that had slanted her story — and could forgive her. Finally he could forgive himself and know his own Shadow qualities, his wife and her shadow qualities, and the love they shared.

What circumstance brings you and your partner to conflict?

What Enneagram traits are evident in your conflict? Are they your Enneagram program qualities or the point to which you go in stress (i.e.,

is this a communication issue or one that will require structural change)? *E.g., My partner is an Eight, usually out front and in charge, but now he's withdrawn, staying late at the office . . . Seems like his stress point, but I don't know what's feeding it . . . AND I refuse to be his caretaker.* Write your version.

Where do you draw the line (i.e., what is your tolerance for open conflict)? *E.g., I think I am tolerant rather than touchy, and I've bent over backwards to make the relationship work. However, if she will not stay with a sobriety program . . . , I'm gone.* Write your own version.

Is there a boundary issue? How close are you now to your limit? *E.g., I need a space of time and quiet. I will not live in a house with constant noise . . .* What history of past successful boundary-drawing has there been between you? *E.g., When the children were little, we worked it out for me to have a separate day off each week. He took care of the kids or paid for the baby sitter.* **Write your own version.**

Are you any better at negotiating your needs with other people? *E.g., You bet. When I was working I negotiated for four ten-hour days, rather than a five-day week, but she thinks I should be master electrician, plumber, carpenter, furniture mover, painter, and galley maid assistant on call twenty-four hours a day . . .* **Write your own version.**

Now the heat is on to do something, anything to stop what seems unbearable. You are in a hurry. Again it is difficult to suffer the slowness of the work of discrimination. Our society that advertises immediate gratification works against us.

Holding onto an image of self as victim and our partner as persecutor is a distortion. When we do this, nothing changes and we do not change.

People in our outer world only confirm or condemn our behavior. Developing a capacity to reflect requires an inner vision not distorted by personal or collective prejudices. So, we attempt to examine our Shadow qualities.

How have you used your partner for your own gain? Your Shadow manipulations?

What feelings and personal needs have you neglected while in this relationship?

Are you using your anger to focus on the issues that need change or just to blow off tension? Do you have a picture of how you would like

things to be? How do you deal with your own aggression? with aggression from your partner? What are you assuming? How might you check this out?

How do you experience your own sexuality? How are you dealing with your partner's? Do you tend to be parent or child in your interplay? How has this become destructive? Do you have a picture of how you would like things to be?

What last straw might you be waiting for? What will you then permit yourself to do?

3

What, who, or where is the current excitement of life for you?

Who are you and what matters most in life to you? How is this restricted in your life with your partner?

What would have to change in order for you to continue in this relationship? in you? in your partner? How have you tried to initiate these changes? What happened? What did you learn would have to shift for the process to work?

What is the neglected transformation element in your Enneagram cluster of traits? Consider its potential impact on your relationship right now. Imagine a situation in which you are facing what you have avoided. *E.g., for a TWO, claiming some separate need that the partner does not see or acknowledge; for a FOUR, the value of the commonplace, perhaps in ordinary human kindness from an unvalued person after a dramatic collapse.*

11

Remembering Self and Completion-in-Union

Use of the Enneagram's rejected element reopens connection to life and a different love of partner.

In the tasks of remembering — bringing old and new parts into our sense of self — we accept and integrate parts of ourselves that previously we have not wanted to know and see. The pain we experience from a current crisis impels us to do the work. It is the impetus to self-knowledge. Memories tell us, not only of pain done to us, but also of pain we have inflicted on others, especially those closest to us. In the example that follows, Ginger woke to find herself in the darkening conflict phase of marriage, when Kurt announced he was moving out. The depth of the pain this inflicted on her was pain Kurt would not let himself feel. It was the pain that impelled her to phase four.

> Kurt, an executive nearing retirement from an international corporation, was used to the perks of an expensive lifestyle. An Enneagram NINE personality type who habitually avoided conflict, he was a competent, easygoing team manager. His sexual affairs had been discreet, he felt, but he was going to miss the irreverent, saucy women, flirtatious and easily available away from home. He began to consider a divorce, but he was "trapped in a marvelous marriage," and he had difficulty making up his mind.
> His wife, Ginger, was attractive, warmly liked by their many friends, an excellent mother, and competent in a garment design business she had developed during their long business trip

separations. He felt no sexual excitement with her, however, and the thought of long retirement years together bored him.

He had no religious background or values conflict, other than that divorce wasn't quite the thing to do. He did not have a woman waiting in the wings, pressing for marriage, although his experience told him he could easily find such a person.

What happened: When he announced that he was thinking of divorce, Ginger demanded that they use professional help to take the time to think and feel why this was happening. She was profoundly shaken. An Enneagram TWO personality, she had placed her primary value in this marriage. She recognized the relationship was not passionate but felt that it had many strengths. During the next year, they both reviewed their early family background, their marriage and family.

Kurt joined a men's group on a "vision quest" that did not improve his view of his marriage but did reconnect him to his western land roots and to his interest in music.

Ginger, on the other hand, worked hard at understanding the crisis she had not chosen but now faced. She read everything she could find, kept a journal, and worked at understanding her marriage and the earlier formative relationship with her alcoholic father. She used individual and group therapy. She lost weight, bought a 4-wheel-drive car and reclaimed her interest in the back-country wilderness. It became clear to both of them that she could take care of her own needs. She had not only reclaimed a spunky part of her earlier personality, but had developed a spiritual depth and a maturity not known before.

Kurt liked her well enough, envied her progress, but still felt "something missing." The therapist became aware that everyone around Kurt (including the therapist) was working hard to supply him with something. Women always had, including the flirtatious women who had supplied the illusion of stimulating sex. What Kurt really hungered for — passionate intensity — he projected onto women and expected them to supply for him.

He needed to reclaim *his own anima* and invest *his own effort* in music, in antique car repair, or in whatever way *he* could find to birth and develop *his own passionate intensity*. He had risked knowing his avoided transformation element of conflict in starting this process, but he had to make it his own through active love. His indolent Enneagram Nine lifestyle would not do.

Kurt began to remember the persons he and Ginger were when they first met.

In remembering the sense of wholeness we once had when we fell in love, we question what is missing from our present life and why. Why are we with our partner, and how does the partnership work? We risk dropping our defenses. We reluctantly look at recurrent questions, recurrently unrecognized in different forms until almost too late. We risk "the alarming possibility of being able."

Like moving through a gate (on one side of which we see only the pain and costs) as we work on these questions, our vision begins to shift. We move through observation to detachment, then to a more inclusive observation. We confront our own power drive, our need to compete. We may have to revisit our root relationships with our parents, with some part that still needs completion and forgiveness. We move then to self understanding. Our capacity to reflect develops an inner vision not distorted by prejudices, personal or collective.

> Even while he did the work, Kurt questioned why he was doing it. He worked with metal and understood the metaphors. This was like plunging metal into a flame until it glows red then white hot; pulling it out and hammering until the crystalline structure grows finer and more supple, until finally it will not crack. Kurt valued his role as a mentor to younger men and to his own children and he understood that what he was learning about the patterns of meaning in his life would deepen this role.
>
> But giving up the dream of a fresh new love was painful. He considered his collection of antique cars. One, a Rolls Royce his own age needed work but it would be great to drive around. On the other hand, it was not as comfortable and practical as their Volvo, or fun like Ginger's Bronco Four-wheeler.
>
> The turning point for Kurt took place in a profound group experience in which he realized the love he had withheld from his family. He called his wife and told her how much he loved her. His work to wake up had begun.

For our wholeness, we need a relationship to fully express ourselves and to suffer the pain that is natural to living. In this way we can achieve consciousness and passion and, finally, we hope we will find love, that multifaceted commitment to our reality with our partner. Compassion and renewed affection emerge, as we stop avoiding our work.

When we remember our past life, we can recognize the transition gates. Some were positive, as when we fell in love. Others appeared only when we had to risk our dreaded Enneagram element — openly expressing anger; feeling needy; failure; feeling commonplace, empty, unacceptable and deviant; feeling pain, weakness or conflict. So many of the gates seem negative.

Like Ginger, we do not choose the event. It makes us feel embarrassed and ashamed. We have a sense of failure and of letting others' expectations of us down. Some pride or self-definition is wounded or destroyed. Then we learn something that we could get in no other way. This wound is the price; this wound is the sacrifice. The ancient Greeks had a saying: "The God sends the wound. The God heals the wound. The God is the wound."

Finally we move through the gate and know ourselves in a new way. We gain the strength, or virtue, that comes from the struggle with our dark side. We behave with here-and-now simplicity; acknowledge the aspects we wanted our partner to carry and the newly discovered parts of our personality — instincts, aggression, sexuality, and strength — as aspects of our own wholeness.

What are you living for and what keeps you from living fully?

How do you differ from your partner? from others? What do you

realize about this? What is the particular strength in your Enneagram cluster? How close are you to mastery?

What is the neglected transformation element in your Enneagram cluster of traits? Consider its potential impact on your relationship, right now. *E.g., If Kurt had risked conflict earlier, his life would have changed.*

Your questions, rather than anyone else's, are your best entry into the issues of your life now. A most surprising exercise is simply to ask yourself 100 questions, writing them quickly on paper, without stopping to answer any. Like a fast scroll forward on a computer, we enter a new realm. It usually happens that we run out of stereotyped, conventional questions after twenty-five or so. Then, as we listen to our inner thought, a new line of questions begins to develop, deeper and more creative.

Try it now. Do not answer any. Just let one question suggest another.

Go well on your journey. *Sample string questions: What is working right about my relationship? When did* _____ *become a priority? Was it my decision? Why did I go along? What am I getting out of it now . . . About 30 questions later: What effect is this project having on (my partner)? Am I creating an artificial crisis to keep up a sense of pressure? What would I have to face if I gave it up? the alarming possibility of leisure? or of not being needed any longer? Am I afraid of the dying of the light or of my creativity? How does this fit with our partnership? . . .*

Everyone with Everyone Else

*The parallel Enneagram process of
the individual and the group—the reality of
a level of communal identity.*

The first part of this book deals with individual behavior, the second with partnership. A third element we must consider is the individual in community.

Enneagram behavior is conditioned and largely unconscious. Most groups reinforce it. Groups induce bonding, repetitive behaviors, and slogans of group beliefs and outlook. We recognize group rituals and drills, but we do not think of friendship routines. We like to be with people who think, feel, and express their convictions the same way we do . We forget that hypnotic patterns can shift the balance from conscious to unconscious behaviors. We lose consciousness more often than we want to know.

The relationship between the individual and the group, the one and the many, has been studied from ancient times, mostly as the military problem of how to create a fighting force. Persians, Greeks, Romans, Nazis, and George Bush's consultants have all used symbol, myth, and pageantry to accomplish their ends. The hypnotic effect of recent televised, yellow-ribbon parades suppressed our consciousness of 85,000 tons of bombs dropped in Iraq. Over 100,000 Iraqi citizens were killed, while only 57 Americans died in the Gulf War. Few Americans question why.

Conscious choice is what makes us human and gives us the ability to create meaning in our lives. We must find a way to retain choice and live in community. Our transformation must take place within this paradoxical arena.

As humans, we share a similar dynamic for transformation of our Enneagram pattern. We move into unconscious Shadow issues, deal with a rejected element, and return with something that shifts our behavior toward greater spontaneity, openness, and a more inclusive consciousness. Yes, but would that it were so simple! The actual process is likely to last a lifetime and takes place within our particular social network of groups and persons who are important to us.

How we resist destructive, unconscious consensual group agreements is a major issue in waking up. How can our work to gain consciousness serve the group?

Most work, friendship, political action, and religious worship, take place in groups, each with its own character. In many ways we can think of these groups as Enneagram types. For example, business associations and the marketplace pop psychology groups are THREEs, most churches are ONEs, the Earth First environmental group is an EIGHT, and the Sierra Club is a FOUR. Not all members in such groups are similar types. Many are opposites and use the groups to balance something in their own lives.

Each group, however, functions as a unit with interacting parts. The group reacts to the conflicting climate of human feelings among its members. It suppresses or uses the rising energies of opposing images—the stable powers-that-be and the creative unknown. Some groups suffer from a systemic distortion, much like the dysfunctional family. When this is so, *talk* about something is blocked. Talking out thoughts and feelings to other members and building on each other's insights to take action is the great strength of groups. It is interesting to know the root word for infantry means "those without speech." Without the power of speech, we are asleep and subject to others' control. "Peace and Justice" groups found themselves silenced when the U.S. bombing of Baghdad began. Simplifying issues of military intervention to "support of our troops" served a cultural addiction to power solutions. Further talk was cut off.

Many groups periodically deal with the Enneagram elements of

transformation they prefer to avoid (powerlessness in the face of the irrational, undefined neediness, rising rage, and conflict while experiencing pain, failure, and the void of not knowing.) To allow the possibility of change, they must continue to say what they sense is true and face outer opposition and their feelings of powerlessness. The group process of bonding, attempting different forms of leadership, and finding ways to work together, resembles that of an individual struggling with his or her Enneagram pattern.

There is a dark side to group influence. Cults, religious and political demagogues, market forces, and forces that mobilize when change threatens, use group techniques to manipulate for their own ends. The Shadow issues of groups are the universal ones, particularly the treatment of other human beings as objects. Group addictions can center on any Enneagram obsession — knowledge and manipulation, helpfulness, vengeance and self-defined justice, security, pleasure, concern with the past, and efficiency. All the defense mechanisms and strengths of the Enneagram that come after wrestling with the unknown are visible in the group process.

Today, research into group process uses general systems theory in its investigations. A system is an organization of interacting parts with a boundary. A community, group, or person is a living system. The individual family member, for example, expresses something for the family as a whole. The disturbed child acts out a difficulty that may originate in the relationship between the parents. Whatever happens to any group member has an impact. Healing in one part of the system affects everyone.

Healing occurs as we take responsibility for our choices. Choices come from convictions. For example, if we believe we can trust no one, we live our lives in this way. If we lose this conviction, we make very different choices. As we find and work with our blind spots, we can help our groups in a similar development to see what they would prefer not to see. We can free ourselves from dysfunctional families by naming the collusions and stopping our part. We can name cultural and economically dysfunctional systems and groups. We can free ourselves from them in a similar way.

An enormous cultural shift is occurring as we approach the Twenty-first Century. Images and feelings expressed in action increasingly invade critical thought. The random, disconnected images of television symbolize it. In computer science, however, there is enormous respect for the particularity of bits of information. We need a synthesizing outlook similar to the disciplined and inclusive vision that comes with Enneagram work.

The swing between the rational and the irrational and between the classical and the romantic, between Apollo and Dionysius is not new to our era. It is a sign that we are in one of the great transition points of human history, similar to the Renaissance and the Industrial Revolution. We are awash with information to sort out. We need to reframe our experience.

It is possible that we are developing a different understanding of the human psyche and how people interact as parts of a group. The famous and the notorious act their ennea-types without self-consciousness, so news stories show the types writ large. Children watch hours of television stories of small groups of people interacting with one another. They grow up to participate in new forms of groups influencing families, churches, schools, even business. All these provide action models, and options. We can quarrel with the limited stereotypes and all-pervasive market materialism, the reduction of great and dreadful events to television drama and the crippling of conversation and political discourse, but something is happening. What we pay attention to, how we take it in, and how we use it is changing.

The forms of creativity have shifted to include group skills. We still have writers and directors, but part of their genius must include knowledge of group creativity. It is more like improv jazz than the classical symphonies. Somehow we rework our structures together in small human-sized groups. A reasonable hypothesis is that we are gaining insight into human motivations and learning how to use it as we go — on the job and in our lives.

Something is happening to the balance of conscious and unconscious forces in our psyches. If we wish to understand the spirit of our times and the meaning of our personal work toward greater consciousness, we must study the interplay of these forces. The mystical traditions in every religious system have always posited an underlying unity among human beings. In many ways, group systems theory does the same. We cannot discount anyone or anything. The issue is inclusion. The question is our imagination. The work we do matters.

It is difficult to know the effect of our individual actions on the larger society, but we each act on our convictions. Consider the following:

FACTS:
1 out of 5 children in the United States is being raised in
absolute poverty in 1991.
330,000 children are homeless.
Suicides among adolescents have *tripled* since 1960.

How do you feel when you read this? What is your experience with poor or homeless children in your community or with a despairing adolescent? Who could help? Do you know if child-protective services exist? Who would you call if a difficult condition came to your attention? How do you feel about a reverse income tax for health and maintenance care

for children who fall below the poverty line? If you believe in this, what action will you take?

Something else we need to care about is the breakup of families (remember the importance and difficulty of our relationship with each of our parents).

FACTS:
There is a 50% divorce rate.
42% of fathers fail to see their children after divorce.

How do you feel when you read this? What is your personal experience with divorce and the children of divorce? What can you imagine would help? Who should do it?

As an individual person, your power to change our societal problems increases when you work with a group or institution that reflects your values. What groups are you aware of in your neighborhood that have the potential to act on your concerns?

How do you find your community?

Oh, not too much. What's new with you?

Afterword

If you wish to send a copy of your responses to any or all workbook segments, we will gather the results and send you a copy of our findings and comments when we finish our study. Send a copy of your pages to:

Molysdatur Publications
203 Star Route
Muir Beach, CA 94965

Do not identify your name on the copy to preserve confidentiality. Send a self-addressed envelope for return of the results.

Glossary

Addiction: An overwhelming desire or need for a substance, object, action, interaction, fantasy, or place that brings about a mental and physical high, or avoids pain. The need is a repetitive and compulsive coping mechanism for conflict, stress or pain. Substance abuse (drugs, alcohol, food) is obvious, but there are are also process abuses, such as workaholism, used to avoid difficult reality.

Anima: Jung's term for a an archetype present in every man, the feminine side. Jung also used this term for a person's inner self that can communicate with the unconscious. ANIMUS represents the masculine archetype, the masculine side of a woman.

Archetype: an inner pattern held in the collective unconscious and possessed by everyone.

Avoidant Personality: A designation for individuals distinguished by their active aversion to social relationships. (Theodore Millon in *Modern Psychopathology*)

Collective Unconscious: Jung's term for that part of the unconscious mind whose contents are inherited and essentially universal within the species.

Compartmentalization: Isolating conflicting thoughts, and feelings from one another in the mind so that one can conceal inconsistent behavior from oneself.

Consciousness: Awareness of perceptions, thoughts and feelings.

Defense Mechanism: Any process by which one protects oneself from recognizing disturbing impulses, instincts, or feelings. Defense mechanisms include projection, repression, sublimation, reaction formation, displacement, rationalization, denial, compartmentalization, introjection, and obsessive thought.

Denial: A defense mechanism of refusal to acknowledge unconscious material which, if acknowledged, would cause painful anxiety or guilt.

Depression: A state of extreme dejection, usually characterized by a feeling of helplessness and the belief that nothing can be done to ease the condition. Sleeplessness, inability to concentrate, a lack of interest in the world, and feelings of guilt can be symptoms.

Ego: The part of the mind with which we identify, the part that makes choices.

Enneagram: A geometric symbol referring to nine basic personality types and their interrelationships.

Esoteric: Something designed for an inner circle of disciples, for the initiated only. A body of doctrine handed down by secret tradition.

Faith: Confidence, reliance, trust. Belief and convictions expressed in character and will.

Hope: To expect with desire, to anticipate with trust and confidence.

Hysteria: Loosely used to refer to neurosis in which the person seems to be seeking attention. A functional disturbance of the nervous system, characterized by anesthesia, convulsion, and disturbance of the emotional and intellectual faculties.

Identification: A defense mechanism in which one fulfills needs by identifying with someone else, of whom he or she is afraid (e.g., "identification with the aggressor").

Individuation: The development of independence and autonomy, an awareness of one's own individuality.

Introjection: The adoption of another person's moral standards, outlooks, and beliefs (usually from our parents).

Isolation: A defense mechanism in which the person deals with painful material by experiencing it without emotion.

Love (Eros, Caritas, Agape): A state of feeling warm affection and attachment to another person, an act of full attention and care that enhances the potential of what the other person can become; in religious terms the affection of God for all creatures. Eros as used by Freud meant the instinct for life. Eros, the masculine God of Love, is associated with sexual passion and the arrows of projection. Caritas is associated with benevolence and care; Agape is associated with shared communal and altruistic love.

Narcissistic Personality: One possessing a set of egocentric traits — strong desire for admiration, indifference to criticism, and an exaggerated opinion of oneself. In its extreme form, the person is totally self-centered, does not care for others, and shows behavior of psychosis and antisocial disorders.

Obsessive-Compulsive Personality: Someone who has high standards and is rigid, meticulous, afraid of making mistakes, and prone to repetitive behavior.

Occult: Hidden or concealed information for the initiated, not known directly by the mind and having to do with the supernatural.

Paranoia: A mental disorder of delusional beliefs. It is not limited to persecutory delusions, although it is often used this way in everyday life.

Paranoid Personality: A disorder marked by extreme distrust, jealousy, and suspicion of others.

Passive-Aggressive Personality: A disorder in which the person resists social demands passively (e.g., by forgetting appointments, being inefficient). Since the person or persons impacted usually feel affronted, the underlying and unacknowledged aggression is evident.

Persona: The outer characteristics of a person meeting society and its demands. Originally meant mask.

Projection: A trait or disposition is experienced as belonging to another person, while its presence in oneself is unknown or denied.

Psyche: From the Greek word for soul, spirit, or mind, as distinct from the body.

Rationalization: Spurious but plausible reasons are produced to explain aspects of one's behavior or feelings.

Reaction Formation: Denying one trait, one expresses its opposite (e.g., one's anger is covered by "sweet reason").

Repression: Unacceptable traits or feelings are unconsciously censored, not allowed into consciousness.

Self: In Jung's terminology, this represents the deepest and most inclusive reality of the person. It has both conscious and unconscious aspects.

Shadow: The archetype representing the unknown and unacceptable aspects of the personality.

Sociopath: An individual repeatedly at odds with society who is unable to form deep relationships, lacks concern for others and is self-centered, irritable, impatient, and incapable of guilt or remorse.

Sublimation: The expression of repressed wishes in an acceptable form (e.g., cruelty turned into a surgeon's skill).

Suppression: Consciously putting an idea or wish out of mind, refusing to act on it. (Contrast with Repression)

Workaholism: (See Addiction)

Margaret Frings Keyes is a social-activist psychotherapist in the San Francisco Bay Area. She has taught and written extensively on crises in the life-cycle and family-legacy questions. She conducts groups for men, women, couples, and other psychotherapists. She also has developed a form of intensive therapy, a ten-day residential "incubation" period, during which an individual works with a current crisis in terms of the Enneagram themes of his or her life.

BOOKS AND STUDY GUIDES
BY MARGARET FRINGS KEYES

EMOTIONS AND THE ENNEAGRAM:
Working Through Your Shadow Life Script

ISBN #1-882042-04-2 . . . . $14.95

"In this refreshingly original and useful guide, Jungian (therapist) Keyes combines the psychological typology of the ancient enneagram with Carl Jung's concept of the shadow. . . . It's a substantial and much needed treatment which broadens the scope of enneagram work considerably. Along the way, the author unpacks the "freightload of distractions, accumulated meanings, and cumbersome speculations" that have clogged the clarity of the nine-pointed diagram. Keyes focuses intensively on mapping the shadow patterns of the personality (the dark, unconscious, rejected, aspects) . . . Beginning in childhood, human behavior crystallizes into one of nine essential patterns . . . each a basic survival strategy . . . Once our shadow issue is identified, we can turn . . . to integration and health."
— Richard Leviton, *East West Journal*

THE ENNEAGRAM CATS OF MUIR BEACH

ISBN #1-882042-01-8 . . . . $9.95

"Ostensibly an enchanting tale of the romance between Aida and Tom-Tom, two cats who live in Muir Beach, *Cats* is a richly layered study of personality types. There are nine types as identified by an ancient Sufi system known as the Enneagram. (Sufism is an Islamic form of mysticism.)

. . . the characters themselves tell their story by showing, not describing, their personalities. You may recognize personalities of people you know in these felines . . . traditional stories such as Abelard and Heloise, Archy and Mehitabel. There is "Silky Su" who gives expert advice on the care and training of cat owners" Delicious, but not exactly a child's story.
— Laura Riley, *The Point Reyes Light*

THE INWARD JOURNEY: Art as Therapy

ISBN #0-87548-368-2 . . . . $12.95

A down-to-earth handbook for using art as therapy. The practical relevance of Transactional Analysis, Gestalt, and Jungian Psychology is presented together with a new supplement by Marie-Louise von Franz on active imagination as understood by C.G. Jung.

". . . it is important . . . I like the lively, concentrated and comprehensive way [the author] throws open a series of doors to a new life . . ." (*Inward Journey*)
— Joseph B. Wheelwright, M.D., Jungian Analyst

"*Inward Journey* by Margaret Keyes is at the top of my list of recommended reading for psychologists, art therapists and educators . . . Her resourcefulness and caring are evident. Anybody who is interested in non-orthodox new approaches can find material here. Because of her eclectic but open minded and discriminating approach, there is much to be learned from Keyes's little book."
— Edith Wallace, M.D., *Psychological Perspectives*

STAYING MARRIED

ISBN #0-89087-902-8 . . . . $14.95

"Drawing on the fascinating experiences of clients in her therapy groups, Margaret Frings Keyes reveals how we can go down into the pain of crises as a source for actual growth . . . a profound examination of ways to keep . . . relationship alive and fulfilling."
— Woman Today Book Club

"This is a book that takes marriage and its problems seriously, written by a woman whose respect for both men and women is obvious. It is excellent."
— Shirley L. Radl, *Palo Alto Times*

THE ENNEAGRAM RELATIONSHIP WORKBOOK

ISBN #882042-08-5 . . . . $14.95

A manual designed to help the reader acquire a taste for enlightenment by consciously entering into states of mind, quite different from his/her own through the use of role reversal. Looking at what is so in our lives is the most practical way of identifying our compulsions. Looking at these same issues through the eyes of different people gives us information and options for change. Includes a self-assessment checklist to identify your Enneagram type.

The second part of the book deals with the partner relationship and marriage. The stages of the relationship parallel the individuation process outlined by C.G. Jung. A series of exercises invite the reader to delve into his or her own life. The book is entertainingly illustrated by M.K. Brown drawings and cartoons.

NEW 1991 LAMINATED CHART/STUDY GUIDES

"Both as a source for individual enrichment and as textbooks for use in Enneagram courses and workshops, I highly recommend Margaret Keyes' approach to the Enneagram."
— Ruth Creighton, *The Enneagram Educator*

ENNEAGRAM PERSONALITIES AT-A-GLANCE

ISBN #1-882042-06-9 (8½" × 11" double-sided) $6.95

Identifies the cluster of character traits associated with each Enneagram point. It names the life-script program, the self-definition, the Shadow issue, the rejected element needed for transformation, the strength that is gained through wrestling with one's personal defects, favorite defense mechanisms, stress responses, and talk style.

The Typeface Key to the Diagram deftly catches the essence of each description. On the overside, the subtypes are developed and Life Script Programs identify the central themes that underlie individual point-life stories.

THE PARTNERSHIP PATH TO SELF-KNOWLEDGE

ISBN #1-882042-07-7 (11" × 8½" double-sided) $6.95

This chart relates the four major stages in marriage: Falling in Love, Role Adaptations, Darkening Conflict, and finally, Remembering Self/Completion-in-Union, to the Enneagram and to the Jungian theory of Individuation. It describes the outer patterns in the relationship, linking them to inner events in the psyche that allow one to become fully individual.

BOOK ORDER FORM
Mail with check or money order to
Molysdatur Publications
P.O.Box 2510, Novato, CA 94948

_____ copies of *Emotions and the Enneagram* . . . . @ $14.95 _____

_____ copies of *The Enneagram Cats of Muir Beach* . . . . @ $ 9.95 _____

_____ copies of *The Inward Journey* . . . . @ $12.95 _____

_____ copies of *Staying Married* . . . . @ $14.95 _____

_____ copies of *The Enneagram Relationship Workbook* . . . . . @ $14.95 _____

_____ copies of Study Guide:
Enneagram Personalities At-A-Glance . . . . @ $ 6.95 _____

_____ copies of Study Guide 2:
The Partnership Path to Self Knowledge . . . . @ $ 6.95 _____

Payment: check or money order:

Subtotal $ _____

Shipping   _____
(add $1/chart; $2/each book)

CA 8% tax   _____

TOTAL $ _____

Send to: (please print)

_____
NAME

_____
ADDRESS

_____
CITY   STATE   ZIP